THE ✥ TIMES

G000143640

getting a TOP JOB in ... the ARTS & MEDIA

simon kent

KOGAN
PAGE

First published in 2001

Kogan Page Limited
120 Pentonville Road
London N1 9JN

© Simon Kent, 2001

British Library Cataloguing in Publication Data

A CIP record for this book is available from the British Library.

ISBN 0 7494 3581 X

Typeset by Saxon Graphics Ltd, Derby
Printed and bound in Great Britain by Clays Ltd, St Ives plc

Contents

1 **Introduction**

Getting a top job in the arts and media is by no means an easy task, not least because there is no simple way to define exactly what constitutes a top job in these industries. It could be the pop star with fame and fortune, the head of marketing at an art gallery, the editor of a magazine or the managing director of a theatre company. All these people could be said to have top jobs in terms of status and reputation, but they are not guaranteed job security or high levels of remuneration. The pop star may have a great rock 'n' roll lifestyle, but unless he or she has sorted out a publishing deal and until revenue from the records start paying back the amount of money the record company has spent promoting, the pop star is unlikely to make a living at all. The editor, marketing manager and managing director may all have key roles in their organisations, but the organisations they work for may be small and so unable to afford much in the way of a salary or employment benefits.

The definition of a 'top job' could be to do with the nature of the organisation you are working for rather than the position you have and the work you do. The programming manager for a local or regional radio station will have less status than someone working in a similar position for a national station. As the profile of an arts or media organisation increases, so too does the level of responsibility connected with the jobs inside those organisations. After all, success and failure in a high-profile organisation will have repercussions that reach further than success and failure in a company with a smaller, regional profile.

Employment structures

To make matters more complicated for this book, while the arts and media industries are closely related, they do not share the

1

same employment structure. Indeed, even within each sector, individual organisations are not managed or structured in the same way. Media companies and organisations certainly have a more recognisable employment structure than the arts in terms of hierarchies of journalists, editors and publication managers. A large media organisation needs the same kind of hierarchy and decision-making structure as any large business in order to operate effectively. There needs to be clear demarcation between the work of separate departments and clarity concerning the responsibilities of each individual employee. There could be a chain of command that governs decision making throughout the organisation. Given this, it is possible for individual media employees to identify a career path and to ascend either through their own organisation or by taking positions of increasing responsibility at diverse organisations. They can become the head of their department, or take a senior management or executive position through determined and committed work for their organisation, picking up the required experience and knowledge of the organisation's market and audience as their career progresses. It is even possible in some large companies to remain employed by them alone throughout your career – brought in as a trainee and developed through diverse departments and levels of the organisation.

In the arts industry, however, no such common structure exists. There's no single acknowledged hierarchy of workers operating across every organisation. A fund-raiser for one company may have a completely different job and remuneration package to a fund-raiser in another. These workers may share a job title but they could be responsible for different areas of their company's work and deal with entirely different people, clients and contacts while carrying out their work. Working for a large, internationally known orchestra or a small touring theatre company will have massive repercussions on the work and consequently the kind of skills and knowledge needed to be successful.

Small organisations

The vast majority of workers in the arts and media sector work for small- and medium-sized employers – organisations of around 300 people and usually considerably less. Regional theatres employ tens of people rather than hundreds. This plethora of small-scale enterprises impacts on both the type of work carried out by employees and the nature of their career progression throughout the sector.

If you work for a small organisation, you are likely to carry out a wide range of jobs or work on diverse projects simply because every employee has to help out with everything. It is a very challenging working environment and requires you to develop and use a wealth of different skills. Working for a small theatre company, for example, will give you experience in all aspects of putting on a production – from securing finance to running the box office. You will need to be extremely flexible in your work – able to take on any new task and have the confidence and ability to work on your own initiative to make sure each task is carried out. At the same time, it is essential for you to be a good team player since you will need to work closely with other people in order to achieve the organisation's goals.

So far as getting a top job is concerned, the main message is that it is up to you to make it happen. You could work extremely hard for your organisation but there may be no way the company can promote you or increase your remuneration because it does not have sufficient resources to do so. If you work for a small organisation and simply wait for others to move on so you can be promoted into their positions, you will not advance your career quickly or effectively. Further opportunities exist in different organisations, different companies and art sectors. It is rare for an aspiring employee to spend more than three or four years in one role before acknowledging that they have done all they can and that it is time to move on to the next challenge. If you do stay for longer, your employer must be able to offer you promotion or new challenges. Accessing the higher parts of the arts sector requires mobility and that means switching between arts organisations, art genres and even geographical locations in order to find the opportunities you need.

Clarity of vision

Thankfully there are an incredible number of locations where arts and media work is carried out. The sector ranges from organisations such as TV and film companies, to live arts venues and even heritage centres and museums. Each organisation has its own targets, its own mission and consequently unique challenges for its employees. Opportunities are there for the taking, but if you are aiming for a top job in the industry, you must be clear about where you want to go.

One record company representative notes that it is all very well receiving letters from people who want to work in the industry, but unless the letter writer gives some indication of what kind of work they want to do in their company it is extremely difficult to offer them a position that they will enjoy and from which they will benefit. Similarly, just saying 'I want to work in films' will get you nowhere because you could end up doing absolutely anything. Saying 'I want to work as a film director' is a much more practical proposition. Now you can identify the things a film director needs to know, the skills they require, and so on. You can then pick out definite roles and work experience needed to become that film director. You will feel that you are gradually building up the knowledge and experience you require to achieve your aim, rather than just watching the industry from the sidelines and getting frustrated because you don't feel a part of it.

With this clear focus on what you want to do, you will be able to move around different organisations and areas of the sector with confidence, gathering the knowledge you need, making the right contacts with the right people and moving your career forwards. It may be that one move you make requires you to take a pay cut, or a drop in your status within an arts organisation, but this may not matter since the experience and skills you are getting through doing that job are beneficial to your overall aim.

If you are determined to be a successful marketing manager in the arts sector, you might switch employment between a visual arts organisation, a theatre and a museum, carrying out marketing duties at each place. By working for a range of different arts organisations you will pick up skills on how to target each art form's individual audience. This in turn will increase your value in the employment market. You could even work in the marketing function outside the arts industry for a while in order to learn how other organisations handle the work and to see if there are any approaches that will transfer into the arts sector.

Freelance working

This nomadic work-style is taken to another level by the enormous number of freelance workers employed by both the media and arts industries. These people do not work for any single organisation or employer but move between individual projects on short-term contracts. They may be film or TV directors, brought in to work for a particular series, they could be artists, illustrators or writers. They could even be freelance marketing managers – PR agencies specialising in promoting theatre performances.

To be successful in this kind of work you must be able to deliver what your customers require, and by making contacts throughout the industry and building a good reputation for yourself, you must create your own work opportunities. Freelance work of any kind involves a significant level of employment insecurity and workers will experience times when there appears to be no work around for anyone as well as times when they are turning work down because they are too busy.

It is extremely rare for someone to start their career as a free-lancer. Usually they will spend time working within the industry, learning about the work and gaining the necessary contacts who will give them work when they go freelance. In some areas of the TV industry becoming a freelance worker is part of the career trajectory. For directors and editors it is expected that you 'earn your spurs' and achieve a level of competence in your field by working with a company at an assistant level before taking the step to the more professional freelance status.

Self-promotion

All freelancers need to promote their own skills, so there's no point in being reticent about your abilities. Some freelance creatives have been so successful at self-promotion that they have achieved success and even fame without an awful lot of talent or content to back up that self-promotion. Certain artists have even been labelled 'careerists' because their work seems to be not so much concerned with making an artistic statement as it is concerned with provoking a reaction from the outside world. This reaction simply serves to increase their public profile and noto-riety, leading to enormous sums of money changing hands for their work. To some extent their behaviour is more like that of pop stars – performers who need to have a strong public image in order to be successful – and they will do practically anything to create that image.

As someone working in the arts or media industries, then, you may not simply enjoy a single straightforward successful career but instead have a series of successful projects. You may be able to enjoy two or three successive careers within the industry, shifting your workplace to match your interests at the time, to reflect your lifestyle priorities or to find new challenges for your skills. If you are determined and successful, you could attain a high position within a specific function of an organisation by the time you reach your early 30s. You could find yourself as head of press and marketing for a high-profile organisation, for example. In this situ-ation you will hardly want to stay doing the same job for the rest of your working life. You may find you can change career course and take on a different role in the arts or find a larger organisation where your skills will be stretched further.

The lateral approach

On the road to success you may find your career stops short for a variety of reasons. It may seem you can never land the job you have your heart set on, the job you feel you can do. In such a scenario the arts industry is wide enough for you to take a lateral approach to advancing your career. You can gain status and respect within the industry through an infinite number of career paths because there is no sense, as exists in other areas of work, that you can only take a top job having spent 20 years working your way up the hierarchy. If you have the skill, determination and opportunity to take on a high-profile job, nothing should stop you from being successful.

In the areas of the industry that demand more creative work, it is extremely difficult to build a secure and continuous career. The fact is that if you want to make or direct TV programmes, write newspaper articles or be creative in some other way, you must accept that there will be less security in your life than if you were to go into more management-oriented roles. At least in management you are likely to be employed full time on a long(er) term contract by an organisation who may give paid holidays and even a pension plan.

Passion

Even if you spend your entire career being employed by major employers, working for the arts and media industries will impact on other areas of your life. The sector works long and exhausting hours to meet demand. Arts workers will therefore find more of their time is spent at work than at home and this is likely to increase the more successful they become. You might put in a full day's work at the office but you still have to carry on working into the night, perhaps providing a public face for your organisation, making sure an event or performance goes well or providing hospitality to special visitors in the audience. Successful performers – be they musicians, actors, dancers or pop stars – will always be in demand once they have secured a level of fame. Journalists must always be ready to file reports no matter what time of the day or night, and if you work as an editor on a business-related magazine you may find a lot of your 'spare' time is spent meeting people from the industry, talking to them about current trends within the sector covered by your magazine. All of these kind of jobs will require your time and energy throughout the week.

A way of life

Working in the arts world successfully demands that you be passionate about your area of work. Workers in these jobs are not merely interested in their subjects – they don't view going to the theatre, cinema or art galleries as an interest, and they don't watch TV just because it's diverting – they do it because it is a vital part of their lives. They need to be involved in the creation of art and in delivering that art to a wide audience. They need to be there at the forefront of their industry, observing what's happening, analysing developments and bringing the latest information or entertainment to the public.

Passion drives people to continue working even if there are dwindling funds or resources. Passion gives people the determination to succeed in spite of the knock-backs they receive – and if you are to work in this industry you must be ready to take the knocks. Making the arts world work is a matter of creative management in itself – there is no option to simply throw money at a problem, you need to find alternative ways around an issue. Passion is why many artists end up staging their own work with no guarantee of financial recompense. This kind of commitment within the industry can also create challenges for those charged with managing personnel. There is a thin line between people doing the work because they get a kick out of it and people being exploited and underpaid for their efforts. Arts managers need to be aware of this and ensure that individuals are not completely taken advantage of by their employers.

Setting the price

To some extent, job insecurity within the industry stems from the unquantifiable value of the products and services in which it deals. While manufacturing companies and other businesses may have clear financial targets and shareholder value to deliver, the targets and values of artistic activities are more elusive. There are some who argue that the arts are a luxury, while others will say they are absolutely necessary to society. But how do you value a theatre performance? You might look at the cost of a seat, and you might compare that to the cost of the scenery, actors' fees and so on, but are you any nearer to being able to state what the value of that performance is? Is opera more valuable because it costs more money? And what would be the value of an art gallery by comparison? Given this, how much should arts workers be paid? Should the director of a theatre company performing well-known work be paid more than a director focused on bringing new work to the public? These are not simply theoretical questions – they do have real implications in the arts world. Without some idea of how valuable an exhibition or a theatre performance might be, a fund-raiser would be unable to negotiate the optimum deal with sponsors of that event. Failure to get the right level of finance through such deals could seriously damage the ability of the arts organisation to operate.

A similar issue exists within the media. No print publication survives solely on revenue from its cover price. In every case it is the advertisers who foot the bill for its production and who provide revenue for the publisher. It is necessary, therefore, to be clear how valuable that advertising space is to specific companies. The value of a page in _Vogue_ magazine will be different to the value of recruitment advertising in the business press, for example. In both cases it is necessary for the advertising executives to determine how much that space is worth. Pitch it too high and you will fail to sell the space. Too low and you will not make sufficient revenue to cover production costs.

Very often the social value of artistic activity is underestimated or entirely forgotten. Art activities can provide a means of expression for everyone – whatever their abilities or background. Art can be inclusive, bringing people together, helping them to share experiences and learn from each other. Art can also be therapeutic, it can be used to develop communication skills and even to overcome trauma. Yet these kinds of projects attract little support from private finance or sponsorship. Corporate funding gravitates towards the high-profile big names, leaving socially conscious art scrabbling for operating funds. And yet in spite of the low levels of funding and the low profile the work might have, the director of a theatre or music company providing workshops based on outreach work can still be said to have a top job in the arts.

Political awareness

Social and political responsibility is an increasingly important factor for those working in the arts and media. From a social point of view, arts organisations are increasingly expected to engage in outreach work, delivering performances and encouraging skills within new audiences or communities where such events do not usually happen. A senior manager of an arts organisation will be acutely aware of this and will have clear ideas as to how his or her organisation can meet such goals. Publicly funded organisations may well find such activities are crucial to their existence – public funds may only be granted if this kind of outreach work takes place.

Political awareness is also crucial if an organisation is to secure public funding on a wider scale. National and local government have different priorities for supporting the arts, and every arts organisation should be aware of new funding initiatives in terms of how such initiatives affect their work. There may be new lottery-based funding practices, for example, where specific projects targeted at local communities receive funding. Skills that enable organisations to tap into these funds are always in demand.

Within the media there is also a need for political and social awareness and responsibility. At a basic level, a reporter on a magazine or newspaper needs to be aware of the legal framework in which they operate. They need to be responsible in terms of the subjects they cover and the way in which they are covered. The increased pressure on journalists to deliver information-rich services 24 hours a day has led to a tendency for some news and feature articles to be dictated by the availability of material through press releases rather than their objective newsworthiness. Successful journalists are those who are able to deliver copy to deadlines, but do not do this at the cost of impartiality or without undertaking professional investigative work. Similarly, within the national press, journalists need to be sure that the kind of interest they bring to a story is justified by its content. There have been too many examples of journalists invading people's privacy and irresponsibly sensationalising an individual's life.

If you are to succeed at getting a top job, you need to understand fully how your industry works and how your own skills best fit into that area. To do this you need to immerse yourself in that sector. You need to know who the important people are, how the sector works, and what the major trends are and will be in the future. You need to get information from as many sources as possible – read the press, network with practitioners in the field and get involved with the artistic activity or the media in question as much as possible. In the early days you may well be working on a voluntary basis, but it is only through gaining knowledge and experience that you can start to command increased responsibility and remuneration.

Lucky you

One major element of getting a top job in the arts is luck. It cannot be denied that being in the right place at the right time will do your career more good than a host of official courses, whether they be dedicated to improving your management skills or your creativity. True, you can sharpen your abilities and improve your impact at work through training, but you still need to get yourself into a position where those skills are acknowledged and appreciated.

However, if you are dedicated and passionate about what you want to do, you can increase your chances of recognition and promotion. Through a proactive approach you can create the circumstances under which you will succeed. You don't need to wait for someone to come up and reward you, you can go and knock on a few doors and take your skills to those organisations. If you have a great idea for an artistic event, go to the people who can help you or who you think should be interested and get them to notice you.

Telling tales

Ultimately, both the arts and the media industries are charged with one activity and that is to tell stories. Throughout the ages human beings have told each other stories – to educate, to entertain or to record past events. The power of stories is constant; the only thing that changes is the medium through which the story is told and the style in which it is told.

If you are working for a national newspaper on a breaking news story, it is clear you need to get information over to your readers in a concise and clear way. Readers will expect a certain vocabulary to be used in the article, and will be used to reading articles of a certain length. Coverage in the national daily press will be vastly different to the same subject covered by a glossy magazine. In TV, a documentary could be created about the same subject, and again the content, style and presentation of the story will be different – a product of the medium used.

If you work as an actor or even a pop star, you are still dealing in stories. You are trying to communicate an idea, an emotion, perhaps an experience through your actions or through your music. If you are making a film or a fictional drama, you are certainly in the business of story-telling, trying to create a plot that will hook your audience, inspire their interest and keep their attention until the end of the show.

By stripping everything down to this one function – to tell stories – it is clear that the arts and media do have a product to sell. It then becomes easier to accept that there is real value to be gained from the media and a real focus for marketing, fund-raising and other administrative functions. This simplification of the work of arts and media organisations may also help you focus on your own career. You may find it is easy to identify what part of the story-telling process your own skills fit into, and therefore what jobs and roles you want to take in the sector.

A new opportunity

This basic focus will not change with the advance of new technology. The high-profile failure of dot.com companies has demonstrated that the Internet is not a dead cert for retail activities. There has not been a sudden or massive switch to Internet shopping for everyday goods, rather it is only when products cannot be bought locally that electronic retail makes any sense. What have been successful on the Internet, however, are content-driven sites. In other words, those sites that provide visitors with information they cannot get elsewhere, or offer entertainment that doesn't exist in any other form. Successful sites are content driven and such sites are already bringing high-profile success to their authors. The Web now provides an ideal platform for creatives to show and share their work. It offers a great place for writers, illustrators, film makers and musicians.

The media and arts world have undergone great changes over the past few years, but there are greater changes to come. The increasing choice of digital TV channels and of Internet-delivered information and entertainment means there are more opportunities for individuals to get themselves noticed than ever before. Competition is fierce within the sector, true enough, but there are fewer and fewer gatekeepers to the industry, monitoring exactly who enters the industry and who stays out. This means that in the world of arts and media the only person who can really restrict your level of success is you.

2 Is this book for me?

Getting a Top Job in the Arts and Media is aimed at you if you're about to embark on a career in the arts or media and want to make sure you get the most from the opportunities offered in this sector of industry. At the same time, it is also of use to those people who are already in the sector and looking for ideas and new initiatives to take in order to develop their career successfully.

For the first of these readers, this book will give a valuable insight into the arts and media sectors through the eyes of those who have already enjoyed successful careers in those areas. Until you actually get involved in the sector it can seem an exclusive and closed place to work. It can feel that you need to be 'in with the in-crowd', know the right people and so on, in order to get your foot in the door. Reading the case studies and learning more about the structure of the industry will enable you to approach your chosen field of employment with more confidence.

You may have a clear idea of where you want to work in the arts and media industry but are unsure of how you can attain that position. You may be certain of an area you want to work in but be uncertain of the precise job you can aim for. You may be unclear as to what experience or skills you need to develop in order to get to that position. In each case, this book will put you in the picture.

If you are already working in the arts or media industry and are frustrated by the development of your career, this book is also for you. By giving a wide view of both industry sectors this book will enable you to see your current situation within the workplace and to identify possible ways to achieve the high-flying role you desire. Working in any capacity within the arts and media is all-encompassing; it can take up your spare time with the need to attend events out of usual working hours and will even preoccupy your thoughts when you should really be relaxing. Working for an arts organisation can entail long hours and low pay, a situation that is not ideal for launching an attack on the more lucrative part of the job market.

The loyalty factor

It can be extremely difficult to find ways to further your career while all your energies are concentrated on fulfilling your current task. Within the arts industry, employees feel a lot of responsibility and loyalty towards their employing organisations. As a result, employees can end up staying at a junior level within their organisation, still happy because their work is contributing directly to the ongoing survival of the organisation, but dissatisfied with the overall position of their career.

Within the media industry, there is also the danger of losing focus on your career while trying to cope with the increasing industry pressures of working to tight deadlines. Any employee producing content for a media organisation – whether it be for a local or national newspaper, for a broadcast station or for a technology-delivered service – can become so involved with delivering that content that they fail to recognise the opportunities for advancement that exist around them or within other organisations. While media workers tend to have a greater career structure to follow than employees in the arts world, they also run the risk of making the wrong choices about career moves, resulting in them being unable to reach the position they desire.

Keeping up with technology

Enjoying a successful career in the arts and media is a considerable challenge for two other reasons. First, many individuals will be employed by small or medium-sized companies. Within such organisations there is little chance of internal promotion and scarce resources for training and development. Second, both sectors are undergoing massive change. The introduction of the Internet and other new communications technologies has impacted on the arts and media world, changing the work and even the workplace irrevocably. Therefore, getting a top job is not about identifying the best job for you to take and aiming for that, but about being aware of the changes currently affecting the workplace, and understanding what they could mean and how they could affect your work in the future. If you are aware of these changes you will stand a better chance of being ready for the top-level jobs of the future than if you aim only to do what is done by high-flyers today.

You may decide you want to be a specialist journalist on a particular subject, but it will not be sufficient simply to aim to take the role carried out by journalists currently in that position. By the time you are ready to take that role, there could be a host of new information channels in operation that you will need to address in order to carry out your work. You will need to adapt your work as these channels develop – deciding how best to exploit the new technology, whether to work for a technology-driven information service, whether to stick with a specialist paper publication, or whether it's possible to do both. In some cases the high-flying jobs of tomorrow simply do not exist today. Similarly, the high-flying positions of today may not exist in 10 or 20 years time – they may have evolved or been replaced outright by changes in the organisation. A current print-based media organisation might expand into Internet and WAP (Wireless Application Protocol) delivery and therefore need a director to oversee these new operations. Even the work of publicity and press officers is changing as they need to address Internet-based publications as well as creating sites to advertise and promote their organisation's work. Moreover, this promotion now has a global angle, since anyone anywhere in the world can access the Web site dedicated to your organisation.

What's the secret?

Just as it is impossible to list a range of top jobs, so too is it impossible to list a series of sure-fire handy hints on how to attain a top job. As will be seen from the case studies that appear throughout this book, gaining status within the industry can happen in any number of ways. It may be that you are able to work for a large media organisation, and follow its internal career development and training programme. However, it is more likely that you will need to create and manage your own training and development initiatives. It should also be noted that many of the people featured in these case studies did not actually start out on their careers with a clear idea of where they would like to end up. There can be few people who decide that they will become director of literature at the Arts Council of England and therefore do every-thing and anything to get that position. More common is that the arts or media worker follows their interests and instincts and discovers these positions as they progress.

There are no rules or easy answers for getting a top job in the arts and media, but there are beneficial approaches – things you can learn from other people and do yourself in order to maximise the potential for your career and place you in the right position for a high-profile job.

So, whether you are about to embark on your career in the arts or media, or you're already getting stuck into working for the industry and need some pointers towards your future, this book offers an invitation to take a step back, to review your situation and put it into the context of wider industry. You can then take positive steps forward to achieve your aims.

How to use this book

Over the next three chapters we will look at areas of work within the arts and media sector: the creatives, the administrators and the management. These three areas of employment have been defined simply for the purposes of this book. Employees within the industry will doubtless object to being classified in this manner and many of them may operate in more than one of these areas, but it enables us to see how employees work together and where the major roles exist within the industry.

Under 'the creatives' we will discuss the work of those who produce the raw material for arts and media organisations. These are writers, musicians, journalists, actors, dancers, and so on. Unlike the other two sections, there are no case studies included for creatives. This is because, first of all, the unique story attached to the success of any creative is entirely idiosyncratic, and frequently bound up with many other influences – from the year in which they started being creative to how one of their friends happened to know someone who knew someone else who helped to launch their career. It would be difficult to use such stories to illustrate any general tips. Secondly, there are many other sources where such case study material can be found. Pick up any glossy magazine or national newspaper and you will find in-depth interviews and features on the creatives who have made it to the top. Interviews with directors, musicians, actors and artists will give you clues and inspiration for developing your own career. Most importantly, you will be able to see from these articles how the creative's particular talents have combined with the Zeitgeist, ensuring popularity and fame.

There are also an incredible number of biographical publications that detail how individuals have achieved high-flying careers. Sometimes written by the creatives themselves, even those written by enthusiasts or fans are useful for getting an idea of how fame can be achieved. There are usually plenty of anecdotes of misfortune and chance, both of which may result in the individual being at the right place at the right time.

Case studies

For administration and management roles, there is more of a hierarchical structure for workers to follow. Consequently, these chapters mix a general appraisal of attaining and working in these roles with a number of case studies. It should be noted that these case studies do not necessarily link directly into the text where they are placed. Sometimes elements of the general text are illustrated immediately by a case study, but equally you'll find case study themes reflected elsewhere in the text.

The case studies are split not only across different roles in the sectors, but across different parts of the industry. The case studies are useful, therefore, not simply for the information about the specific job the individual is doing now, but for the progression they made in order to attain that position and the views they hold of the sector in which they work. If you are interested in the broadcast media, don't simply read Lorna Clarke's case study of working at BBC Radio 1, take in as well Jeremy Mills – the co-director of independent production company Lion TV – and Mark Thompson – Director of Television at the BBC. If you want to work in the music business, you should read about Charlie Harris, a director at Serious Records, Helen Nattrass, a personnel manager working at EMI UK and Ireland Ltd, and Karen Cardy, a publicist working in the classical music sector. There are four case studies concerning publicity and press-oriented roles, but these are situated in visual arts, the theatre, classical music and at an arts venue. All four contain useful information about press and publicity work while also containing information relevant to each artistic area.

The indirect route

Success in the arts and media industry often occurs through indirect routes, when individuals take a lateral approach to the use of their skills and the jobs they do. Take the same approach when using these case studies. By gaining a range of perspectives on working in the industry you will understand how the sector works, and the attitudes of those who have already achieved a high level of success in their area.

Having described the sector from an employment point of view, Chapter 6 then considers what key skills are required within the sector and how to go about getting those skills. There is then a short chapter highlighting where to look for these top jobs, which will inspire you to take positive steps towards the development of your career. Finally, the Appendix contains useful addresses and particulars of Web sites. This section not only indicates places to go to increase your skills and find new opportunities, but also offers some key information sources that you can use in order to ensure that you keep in touch with developments in the workplace around you.

3 *The creatives*

For the purposes of this book, the general title of 'creatives' refers to those people in the arts and media industry who instigate artistic events, programmes and art works. They provide content for the media – journalism in print, reporting for the broadcast media, and so on. They are artists, actors, dancers, writers, singers – people who perform or create material that is the starting point for an artistic event. These are the people who dedicate their lives to making an impact through their creative talents.

In this area there is the chance to be extremely successful, to earn a great reputation for your work and enjoy a high-flying career. However, recognition can take some time to arrive and the frustration experienced by many creatives on the way results in them giving up and finding something else to do with their lives. Persistence can, and frequently does, pay in this area, but it does not always pay enough at the right time. It is also the case that in this area of work both the arts and media sectors are biased towards the young – in terms of audience and employees. It is extremely rare for a new pop star to achieve fame having already reached their 30s, and it can sometimes seem as if both the print and broadcast media are obsessed with delivering new products purely to the 16- to 25-year-old age group. But while success may be more of a challenge for more mature creatives, it does not mean it is impossible.

There is no simple answer as to why some creatives are successful while others languish in obscurity. Each success story is unique, just as every successful artist is loved for their individuality and originality. However, there are certain qualities shared by creatives across artistic and media genres and certain approaches that have taken them towards success. In general, there are two principal elements to getting a successful creative artistic career, elements that may even prove more important to success than talent. These elements are determination and luck.

Determination

There can be no doubt that the most successful actors, musicians and writers today have achieved their success through single-minded dedication to their work. They have usually decided what they want to do at an early age and pursued their goal through activities at school and college. Classical musicians will already be accomplished and receiving professional training in their teens, pop musicians will have been in a number of bands throughout their adolescence, writers will have ploughed their way through reams of paper. Success happens because, to some extent, these creatives have not allowed for the possibility of anything else to happen. All their energy has gone into becoming successful because there was never anything else they wanted to do – they refused to compromise their ambitions or be deterred by people telling them it would be too difficult and they should concentrate on getting Plan B into shape for when it didn't work out. Instead, they just went ahead and did Plan A.

Unless you are remarkably lucky you will not immediately strike gold and receive big pay cheques. Even so-called 'overnight successes' conceal a history of previous failed attempts, potentially embarrassing past jobs, and long nights of the soul when the creative concerned questioned whether anything good would ever happen to them. There are examples of this all around – indeed, entire TV shows have been constructed from the early inauspicious appearances of celebrities – a future Spice Girl modelling the prizes on a Turkish game show, Nick Hancock and others appearing in bad TV advertisements, and so on. Creatives involved in all areas of art will have been through a great deal of hardship in order to achieve their success. Because they haven't invested in Plan B they may have endured times of poverty or difficult living. But instead of being disheartened, these hardships have simply added more drive and determination to their work.

Flick through the biography of any pop star, actor or writer and you'll find a catalogue of disasters that makes you wonder why they didn't give it all up and go for an easy job at the bank. Musicians undertaking endless tours of dodgy pubs in the back of a clapped out transit van, actors working ridiculously long hours to put on a play at a small venue that might get some attention from the press or an agent. The stand-up comedian who has spent 3–5 years traipsing around the comedy circuit in London and across the UK having things thrown at him but carrying on regardless.

Self-belief

Ultimately, the only thing that will see you through these periods is your own self-belief and complete conviction in your abilities and what you are doing. In the arts, unlike any other industry, no one particularly wants you to do what you want to do for a living. No one is ever going to come up to you out of the blue and ask you to write a song or to play Hamlet. You have to make them come to you. You need to get yourself into a position where people want you to play, dance, write or act, but that will only happen when you've demonstrated what you are capable of and why your unique skills should be delivered to a wider audience.

Self-belief has to be at the centre of your work. You'll experience times of doubt, but as long as there remains a feeling that what you are doing is right and that it is only a matter of time before other people realise your talent, then you are on the right road to getting the attitude required for success. Hold on to that feeling with all your might. Learn to trust that conviction and use it to guide you. It will constantly be under attack from other aspects of your life. There will be financial pressure for you to get a better paid 'proper' job as you need to pay the household bills. There could be further pressure from friends and family who expect you to have achieved a certain standard of living by a certain time and who may never truly understand what you do for a living.

As mentioned above, every success story is unique and so the career trajectory for every individual will be different. Some creatives may have trained through college to be professional musicians, while others could be self-taught. They may spend their early career unemployed, but still obsessively practising their skills. Whatever path you take, it is clear that you can't starve while waiting for the big time to strike. You need to find a way of supporting yourself so that you can pursue your goal. It's a difficult balance to find, as essentially you are after an activity you can do that will finance your lifestyle but will not take up so much of your time that you are no longer able to work on your creative career. The reason why so many struggling actors and actresses can be found waiting tables is because this work enables them to take time off for auditions and rehearsals. It may not pay well, but it pays enough, is flexible and if they do get an acting job for a few weeks, they can drop the work and pick it up again afterwards. Try doing that if you're employed by a bank.

Luck

Determination is an attitude that is completely under your control. You can decide whether you believe your life work will succeed and how confident you feel about what you are doing. Luck, on the other hand is, well, luck. However, this is not to say that you cannot have some influence over the chances available to you. There are a couple of often-quoted clichés concerning how to be a successful creative in the arts and media world. The first is that you need to be in the right place at the right time and the second is that it's not what you know but who you know that counts. Both are true, and in each case you can be proactive to make the rules work for you. Put simply, you can do things that put you in the right place at the right time and you can get to know the people who could prove key to your creative success.

Making your own luck is a matter of self-promotion. If you want to be taken seriously in your chosen field, prove you can do it in front of the people who matter. You can increase your chances of success simply by creating more opportunities for your work to be recognised. Rather than expecting your writing work to be accepted only by the BBC, research and send ideas to one or two of the many independent TV production companies that now exist. Whether you intend to write drama, comedy, or want to create your own documentary programme, these independent production companies will offer you more contacts within the industry and therefore more opportunities for work. If you've written a novel and are waiting for an agent or publisher to get back to you, use the time to write something else. Put together another idea or proposal that you can send off elsewhere. If nothing else, when the big time does come you will have a library of ideas you can offer to other publishers. If you're in a pop group, don't just keep plugging away at the same venues on a regular basis. Find new ways to promote the band – try radio stations, national music programmes, local news or arts programmes. Be prepared to approach anyone and everyone who might be interested in your product.

Showcase your talents

Put on a show, an exhibition or an event to showcase your talents. Promote the event to the public and the industry. Get the media on board, plan it, design it, push it to your audience as effectively as possible. In some parts of the music business, this in itself can be enough to put you on the road to success. If you want to be a successful DJ or club promoter, staging an event off your own bat will immediately demonstrate your talents and provide ample feedback as to what the audience think of your work.

Making the most of these events means guaranteeing that the people you need to impress turn up to see it. This can be difficult, especially if you are a relative unknown, but there are many ways of providing enticement. You might make promises of free hospitality, drinks, food, and so on. You might try getting a currently well-known artist in your area to come on board and put their name to the project. Consider setting up a music gig, a comedy gig or a club night and book a well-known figure from the industry as the main attraction. In this way you can guarantee audience and industry interest, which then reflects on your own artistic activities when you appear alongside the star. This could be expensive, of course. Not only will you be expected to pay artists' fees, but you will have to demonstrate that the event is of a high quality. Stars are cautious about the shows they accept and where they appear because they don't want to damage their own reputation or cheapen their appeal. You should maintain a sense of balance throughout organising the event – when you've achieved fame and fortune, would you be happy to appear in a show like this?

You may be able to get a well-known visual artist to comment on your work or exhibit as part of your event. You might be able to attract a more accomplished actor or director to work on your play

– very often, established artists will get involved with lower profile projects because it offers them an opportunity to do something different, to experiment with their own work and expand their skills. In recent years there have been a number of well-known film celebrities taking part in West End and even fringe theatre shows – attracted by the idea of showing the audience that they can really act. You may not be able to attract headline stars, but even an actor who brings along a couple of agents and a reviewer will be a positive move.

Networking

Crucial to success with such events and to building a successful artistic career is networking. Many people regard networking as a horrendous thing to have to do. It has negative connotations of crawling to people, of using flattery and insincerity in order to get people to like you and to do things for you. In reality it is simply how the industry works. It is part of day-to-day life. There's nothing sinister or underhand about it – it is simply the case that employers in the industry will work with people who they know and trust. Thankfully, networking is not something some people can do and others can't. It is a skill that anyone can develop.

On the one hand, networking is simply the act of talking to your mates, telling them what you're doing and seeing if they or someone they know wants to get involved as well. On the other hand, it's about walking into a formal gathering or meeting and specifically approaching people who you believe can help your career. In both cases the approach and effect are the same – you are talking to the other person primarily through a shared interest. Your secondary reason is to seek their knowledge, guidance or help with your work. You don't wade in there and immediately tell them what you do and what you want, but through a casual discussion you uncover ways to help each other on a mutual basis. You show an interest in them, they will show an interest in you. Even if the person you are talking to doesn't have anything you need or can't help directly, networking can raise your profile in a positive way within the industry. You might find yourself chatting to a member of the press after a performance or at a private view in an art gallery. You may not have an event for which you need immediate coverage but simply through your meeting you will know who to send publicity material to and they will know who you are when they receive it. It may even mean you are able to phone the press contact and talk to them directly about your project rather than communicating through press releases as everyone else does.

The art of networking

Networking in the arts industry is easier to do than in other business sectors. Many business sectors have official and unofficial barriers to entrance – professional qualifications, seniority within an organisation and so on – that must be met before you can talk to the people who matter. The arts industry is open to anyone. At any single arts event there may be highly qualified academics, artists straight from school, practitioners in their 40s and 50s, arts organisation directors and company secretarial staff. Because art is a subjective matter, all these people can talk to each other and share their views regardless of background. They are united by an interest in visual arts, classical music, pop music or the theatre and everyone's view is valid.

In addition, arts workers do not usually work in direct competition with each other. There's a sense of goodwill and encouragement for people who want to put something on, rather than any suspicious feeling of someone stealing audience or revenue from their own projects. Even when one actor gets a part over another, resentment is often tempered by the feeling that they got the part because they were more suitable and not because they were better or more talented. Of course, there will always be some people who are exclusive rather than inclusive of newcomers, but if so, ask yourself if these people are really of use to your career anyway? Are they regarded as the last word in the area you want to work in or can you achieve success another way?

Creatives in the media world have no less need for networking even though the more clearly defined hierarchy of employment in this sector means there is a more straightforward path to promotion. To maximise your chances of success, you need to network in two ways: first among the industry or interest area you are writing about, and secondly across the media industry itself, ensuring editors and managers are aware of the skills you have.

Gaining trust

Specialist journalists, who report in detail on one particular subject, can offer their skills and knowledge to editors at a much higher price than general journalists. However, you can only secure this kind of knowledge if people within the industry know and trust you and therefore enable you to source breaking news stories or to get the detail on important issues. As a leading journalist in your particular area, you may spend much of your time simply talking to people in the industry, gaining their trust and working with their opinions.

Many national newspapers take columns from celebrity and specialist writers who work on a freelance basis and receive great financial reward for their published thoughts. Achieving this kind of notoriety requires the same approach as a popular music artist. On the one hand you need to prove you are skilled and determined in your written work. On the other hand you need to demonstrate a unique selling point – a clear idiosyncratic approach that marks you out from other journalists and writers, guaranteeing that editors will want you. This unique selling point may have nothing to do with specialist knowledge and everything to do with your profile – whether you're a staunch supporter of the status quo or a _bête noir_.

There is no simple or straightforward way to becoming a high-flying columnist in the national press. Every opinion former or commentator in every paper has made their way in a different manner. Some have news reporting backgrounds and through this work found opportunities for TV work. This in turn has led to presentation work on other programmes or work in other sectors of the media, forever increasing their profile. Others may have taken an academic route. They may have published important works of cultural analysis, clearly staking their territory as important spokespeople for the current generation. Alternatively, journalists may have been working on a publication that suddenly achieved high status due to its importance within the culture of the time. Journalists may find success through writing about a certain type of music that becomes a phenomenon, or reviewing computer games that take over the nation's psyche. In practically every case, however, columnists will have already achieved fame and notoriety before they are asked to write a weekly piece for the national papers.

Take aim

How can you increase your own chances of attaining similar status? To begin with, you must bear in mind that the print industry still maintains boundaries between different types of publications. In TV there is increasing convergence between fact- and fiction-driven programmes. Documentaries are blending with dramas, with quiz shows and other formats to create new entertainment shows. Consequently, the people who worked only on documentaries, for example, are now finding it easier to move to other areas of TV output.

In the print sector, however, there are clear distinctions between people who work for the trade or business press, the national press and the glossy consumer or lifestyle magazines. The chances, therefore, of being able to work for a business publication and then move to a lifestyle magazine, or even the national press, are extremely slim. As a result, when starting out on your career – and indeed at every stage along your career trajectory – you must be clear of the area of the press you want to write for and aim to be involved only in that area.

If you want to be a high-flying news reporter with the national press, you can still achieve this by starting out as a reporter on the local paper and working your way up. It may even be possible to secure a training scheme position with a national newspaper and start to work in this part of the media immediately, but you will not help your cause by diverting into the business press, even if the job represents a promotion for you. Similarly, if you want to write for one of the glossy lifestyle magazines, get work with a publishing company specialising in this area. Writing, in terms of style and content, is immeasurably different in these publications compared with other parts of the print media. Articles are of a different length, require a different level of detail, a more accessible and chatty style, and usually a strong visual angle for good

28

7777

7

photography. Working for a publication that does not share these priorities will not help you into the higher positions with your target employers. Training in the local press does not outcast you from working in consumer magazines, since it is still accepted that the local press offers an effective training ground for any journalist, but it would be a mistake to go into any other area of the press subsequent to this if you want to work in the lifestyle sector.

Self-publishing

In today's technology-powered print industry it is more than possible for you to launch your own magazine. You will need good financial and commercial backing, but if you identify a niche market – an opportunity to address an audience of readers not currently served – you can write and design a magazine from a couple of computers. To do this you will need a whole host of other business-related skills, and may need to bring a few other people on board to make the idea work, but this need not deter you. Magazines make most of their money through advertising sales, so while you may be motivated by the idea of writing about a subject you know well, you must also consider who will read the publication and subsequently who will want to advertise to that readership.

Getting in

Very often creatives are disheartened by the apparent inaccessibility of large arts organisations. They'd like to get into the BBC and start making programmes, but there's such a bureaucracy and sense of an 'in-crowd' that it appears no one is interested in new ideas from unknowns. The fact is, arts organisations are constantly on the look out for new talent and strong ideas. You may not be 'in with the in crowd' now, but it is only by approaching these people that you can make the contacts necessary for success. Sometimes a lack of knowledge about how an arts organisation operates can even work in your favour. If you don't know how the bureaucracy works then you don't need to follow the 'right way of doing things' when contacting that organisation. You can be completely maverick in your approach, as long as what you offer is strong and you are clearly capable and dedicated to delivering that work. If there is quality and conviction in your work, then any arts organisation will want to work with you, regardless of how they operate and how much or little you know about their operations.

You don't know how TV programmes are financed? What does that matter? If your programme idea is strong enough there will be people within the organisation who will sort out the financial side. You didn't realise you should have submitted your work to one of the editorial assistants on a magazine rather than the editor him- or herself? What does that matter? The editor has seen your name pass across their desk. They may even read the article and pass it on with a note to their assistant to follow it up. Innocence – rather than ignorance – can be beneficial. Clearly you need to make sure that the organisation you are approaching could be interested in and develop your work, but how they realise your ideas or process the decision to go ahead with your work is neither here nor there. If you have a startlingly original idea that they like, then your lack of administration knowledge is irrelevant.

So go ahead – knock on a few doors and show them what you can do. Convince organisations that your talents are important and demand to be recognised. Never be intimidated by the organisation you are approaching, otherwise you will always be considered as subservient, a bit-part player in the arts and media world, rather than the leader you want to be.

Being the same, only different

For some artists, the road to fame and fortune began way before they had to think about making a living. Performing or creating art while still at school or college offers the freedom to experiment and to promote your own art without the immediate need to meet financial responsibilities. This is still the case even though student loans have put an incredible amount of pressure on students to find lucrative work as soon as they leave education. If you are a student going into further education, you should not let financial considerations compromise the opportunities that exist, for even at this time, self-promotion activities are possible, and can prove crucial to your future success.

In recent years a number of visual artists have achieved noto-riety almost immediately after leaving education. They have mounted their own exhibitions, frequently in new spaces opened and managed by themselves. They successfully inspired the interest of critics, art collectors and the public. Whether the press or important people in your own part of the arts world recognise and accept your activities as valid or remarkable is a chance you have to take, but there are two ways you can improve the chances that your efforts will be recognised.

The first way is to make sure your work is contemporary and relevant to today. You may not be able to create an entirely new artistic movement, but if your work is a reaction to or continuation of styles, issues or ideas that have gone before, there is a greater chance that you will gain people's attention. If you aim to achieve a high profile, you should already be fully aware of current trends in your field, and indeed you should find that your work fits natu-rally into this scene.

The second element of the equation may seem to work against this contemporary theme, but it is to be different. Be unique. No one will be interested if all you want to do is repeat precisely what has gone before. It may show you to be a good technician, in possession of fine skills and talent, but it doesn't show that you have any promise in terms of taking the art form further. Moreover, if you are simply one of many other people with the same idea, trying to fill the same space in the market, you'll find yourself spending all your energy trying to beat the competition rather than striking out on your own and breaking new ground.

These elements apply whatever field of art you are working in. You may be trying to produce attention-grabbing visual art, launch your pop group, begin your acting career or stage your own play. In every case do something different that people will not have seen before but which they feel they must see and be a part of because it could easily be the next big thing. More than half the battle for a successful artistic and creative career lies in promotion and hype. If you can pitch yourself and your art in the right way, issues of quality or originality may not matter so much. If you can convince critics, and consequently the wider public, that what you're doing is important and intrinsic to the future of your art form – be it performance, music or film-making – then the media will start looking to you as a reference point in the coming months and years, regardless of your actual output or performance.

The main event

What kind of events will get you the opportunity you need to show the outside world what you can do? What performances or exhibitions can you create that will attract the people you need to attract? Again this will depend on your art form and the kind of impact you need to make. If you're in a pop group you may decide the way ahead is to create huge local support for your act that will secure a level of popularity that makes it impossible for the wider industry to ignore you. Alternatively, you may decide you need to be strategic about where you play, performing a small number of gigs at high-profile venues where you are guaranteed press coverage and the appearance of record label representatives. There may be competitions you can enter – certainly in the area of literature there are many competitions for poetry, stories, novels and plays by unpublished writers that can result in your gaining an increased profile and therefore a top-level publishing deal.

The long haul

When embarking on your chosen creative career you must commit yourself to the long haul. You cannot expect your first stab at fame to succeed. Your first audition will in all likelihood be a complete disaster. The first time you try DJing you might clear the dance floor. The important thing to remember throughout this time is that you are learning from experience. Whatever event you put on, however many people do or don't turn up, there will be valuable lessons for you to learn that will inform you about how to go about future projects and how to make things better.

Each time you complete a project, an event or a performance, ask yourself what was good and what was bad about it? What did people enjoy and where were the problems? When you stage your own play it becomes clear whether the show is funny, moving or incoherent in a way you can never tell from reading it yourself or receiving feedback from other readers. You may get half way through writing your novel and hit writer's block, but you can't just stop there, you must learn how to work past the blockage. Even if what you end up writing is substandard, you need to develop the discipline to succeed, to work hard and achieve your aims.

Realistic targets

In these early days don't set your expectations too high. Your overall aim can be achieving fame and fortune – fine, that is your prime motivation – but in the short term your targets should be realistic and practical. Aim to have your screenplay finished by the end of next month. Aim to have made a low-budget short film by the end of 10 months. Aim to have written three articles on spec for a lifestyle magazine by the end of the week. By achieving these targets you will be able to draw greater confidence in your abilities, and once you have confidence in your abilities you can inspire confidence in others that you are up to the job.

Remembering you are in this for the long haul is also key if you are to ride out the disappointments in your chosen career. There may well be examples of individual artists who have gained success at an early age, but you can still be a good and recognised artist later in life. There is no time at which you officially become too old to be creative. You may have to find new channels for your creativity, but that is also part of your own development as an artist. In other words, you can have a successful and developing creative career without the overblown fame and hype afforded to household names. Indeed, achievement with a lower profile can be far more satisfying – not least because you don't need to sacrifice your private life in order to maintain that popularity and success.

Keep your own artistic achievements in perspective and you will constantly find new ways to practice your art and new opportunities to do what you want to do. Your pop group may enjoy limited success throughout your early 20s, you may find some band members leave as they become disillusioned and decide they need a job with security and a decent, reliable pay packet.

You, on the other hand, may find you can play in more venues as a solo artist and that it's a lot easier to manage your musical output on this basis rather than having to deal with comments and suggestions from everyone else.

As an actor you may have come out of drama college and got precisely nowhere apart from a couple of commercials, a corporate video and seven years waiting tables. As you get older, you might find your face suddenly fits. You may not have been the right person for all those young romantic leads, but suddenly you are just the right person for the older, more thoughtful or more comic roles. So while in the short term you must be completely focused and dedicated to the projects you are involved in, over the long term your focus should be on the wider artistic world. This month you are focused on playing a role in a short film, but in the wider frame you are looking for acting work in the theatre, TV and feature films. Today you will finish writing a chapter of your novel, but in the long term you have several ideas for TV programmes.

Net benefit

The Internet now offers another platform for creatives of all kinds. Writers can use Web pages to promote their own writing, demonstrating their style and ideas. However, the multimedia aspect of the technology means film makers, musicians and visual artists can all use the Internet to promote their work. This new medium has already launched some high-flying creative careers. The creators of one spoof TV review page have since been brought in to work on comedy shows on TV. Film makers have had their work spotted on the Net, and in one instance a group of actors plus production crew made a complete episode of a situation comedy, using the Internet to make it available to anyone with the appropriate technology to download the show.

The only drawback of doing things off your own bat is finance. To begin with, you might be able to beg and borrow equipment, skills and even finance from your network of friends and colleagues. You might be able to offer benefits in return – a VHS copy of the film you're making, front-row seats in the theatre when the play is staged, a copy of the book or a mention in the credits when it is published. Take a lateral approach to the problem – find people who might not normally be involved in financing the arts but could be inspired by the idea. You might even secure a lucrative sponsorship deal with a company from outside the arts industry.

However, no matter how many people in your network are happy to work for free or donate equipment, there is bound to be some cost involved somewhere – whether you are publishing, film making or staging a play in a theatre. Even then there are a number of different ways you could find the finance you require. First of all, there may be arts awards or grants available for your project. Make enquiries at the Arts Council, your regional arts office or through other organisations dedicated to your field of practice. Secondly, there is self-finance.

Raising the cash

Self-financing can mean slaving away for months at a crummy job that pays well, in order to save up enough money to fund your creative project. You might hate the job, but it means you build up funds to support you while you write, act or direct. On more than one occasion a film director has financed his own movie with money earned by taking part in a medical experiment for a pharmaceutical company. There are also examples of creatives funding themselves through their own credit cards. This is a particularly high-risk approach – the idea being that the project will be enough of a success to meet the money they ended up owing. However, it is also a mark of how seriously the creatives take their work and how certain they are of their own ability and success.

While some creatives have attained success by identifying what they wanted to do and going out to do precisely that, there are other creatives who have found success almost by accident. For some, they have not particularly been looking for success, but found it comes to them anyway, through chance and fortune. For others, fame has appeared from a completely unexpected source. While trying to write for one programme, a TV writer was spotted by a different producer who offered them work. Having become disillusioned with the number of auditions they were failing, an actor decided to put on their own show, only to have incredible success with the show that set up their career for the next five years or more. In these cases, however, it is clear that fortune only occurred because the creatives involved were ready and able to take advantage of the situation as it presented itself.

Ultimately, if you have conviction in what you are doing and the determination to see it through, you will find a myriad of paths around the problems you face. Finance, time, lack of resources will all pale into insignificance as you pursue your artistic aims. This is what makes you successful as an artist – not whether you immediately make money and receive accolade upon accolade, but whether you are still able to do what you want to do in your chosen field. If you are still able to act, write or create art in whatever way, without completely starving in the process, then you are a successful creative.

4 *The administrators*

The broad title of administrators is used here in reference to those employees who have a hands-on role in keeping arts organisations running. They may be managers concerned with the running of a particular function within an organisation, charged with seeing that projects are completed on time, and that the work of the creatives and other employees are managed and remunerated properly. They will also work to see that new initiatives or strategies instigated by senior managers are acted upon.

Within the arts sector, these roles include work such as press and publicity, marketing and fund-raising, box office management and even company management. Administrators may be responsible for arranging tours, sorting out accommodation or transport, and ensuring each element of a production is in place on time. I am stretching the definition of administrators to include other media roles such as editing and production management in the print media, and production, editing and directing roles in broadcasting. While these roles are not really administrative tasks, they do fall between entirely creative roles on the one hand and pure management tasks on the other. This work involves the shaping of raw material to create programmes or publications. There are strong organisational and management skills required in such roles as well as a good deal of creativity and, in some cases, specialist knowledge and skills.

In both the arts and media sectors, administrators may work in the more general business-related functions of an organisation such as finance or personnel administration. In larger companies, the fact that you are working within the arts world may be irrelevant to your day-to-day activities. Your aim is to ensure the accounts balance or that the human resources needs for the organisation are met. In this way the work of your organisation can continue.

Viewed from one perspective, these roles may be considered simply as a stepping stone on the way to a real 'top job' in senior management. From another, they can be high-profile jobs in themselves. The head of personnel or head of marketing for an arts organisation may not want to move any further up their organisation's hierarchy. Their skills and ambitions are satisfied by excelling within their particular function. Job seniority depends on the area of work and the structure of the employing organisation. The company manager of a small theatre company may be considered to be at the top level of his or her organisation, whereas the company manager for a touring show produced by a larger theatre would simply be another part of the junior management team.

Same job title, different job

The concept of seniority is further complicated in this area of work since the levels of responsibility and remuneration afforded to similar employees in different organisations varies incredibly. In some large theatres, the role of development officer may be a strategic one involving liaising with a range of people from different functions in the organisation. In a smaller company, a person with the same job title may simply be involved with hands-on fund-raising duties. In some organisations roles may be combined – thus the tour manager for an orchestra is responsible for press and marketing as well as managing the logistics of the tour in terms of accommodation and travel. In each case, remuneration is likely to be a factor of the profile and financial position of the employer, rather than the individual's level of responsibility.

Many of these administration roles involve bridging the gap between arts organisations and the creative artist him or herself, a role that requires expert people skills and a blend of business skills. On the one hand these workers need to understand and appreciate the work and interests of the artist, ensuring they are happy with the way their work is promoted, or the way they are treated by other people in the organisation. On the other hand, there are targets to be met by the organisation itself in terms of audience attendance or other forms of revenue. This balance is affected by the type of art the organisation is dealing with. Within a record company, for example, there is far more emphasis and focus on pushing a definable retail product to customers, whereas an exhibition in an art gallery may be more about raising awareness of an artists' work. The work will also be affected by whether the artist concerned is living or dead. There is a world of difference between promoting a gallery event by an artist who is willing and able to get involved in promotional activities and promoting an exhibition of work by a past master. In the case of the latter it does not necessarily mean the arts administrator has an easy ride. The estate of an artist will be just as concerned to maintain the image and reputation of the artist and will want to ensure that every aspect of an exhibition is fitting.

Organisational structures

Media companies often have a more recognisable organisational structure for administrators to work in than their counterparts in the arts industry. Having spent time working as a reporter, an employee will see that the next step up is to assume some level of editorial control. While this is clearly a promotion, media workers make a clear career commitment as to where they see their work leading when they make such a move. Once you have taken an editorial position it will be more difficult to change the type of publication you are working for, and it will certainly reduce the amount of actual reporting and creative writing work you carry out. However, just as some arts employees are satisfied to excel in their particular functions, some publication editors view their job as the height of their career. This is certainly the case for editors of magazines that enjoy a high profile, that may be considered to be at the cutting edge of contemporary culture or the vanguard of opinion for a certain industry.

To succeed in these roles – whether they are your ultimate objective or simply another stage in your brilliant career – you must be clear about one thing: you do this work because it is what you want to do and not because you are a frustrated creative artist who's doing this until they are discovered. These jobs entail a heavy workload, irregular hours and a great deal of pressure. They are often placed at the point where artistic activity meets financial limitations, and where commercial sense and innovation go head to head. For this reason there are often points of friction, areas where critical and sensitive negotiation is necessary to find a solution. Without a passion for the sector of the arts or media you are working in, and without a great deal of self-motivation towards the objectives of these roles it is unlikely that you will enjoy these jobs or be particularly successful.

Pim Baxter – Press and marketing in the visual arts

Pim Baxter's career in the arts didn't really start until after she had had a family. While looking after her young family she took an Open University degree, which gave her a wide range of contact with the arts, from poetry and visual arts, to drama and literature.

Having decided that drama was her greatest love, she secured a job in the Friend's department of Kent Opera, moving on to the post of education officer for the company before taking a press job at The Orchard Theatre, Dartford – one of the touring venues visited by Kent Opera. The Orchard is a receiving house – meaning it takes in productions from companies rather than creating performances itself. This meant Baxter was involved in promoting a wide range of shows to her audience and was forever trying to get press coverage in the local media.

This proved to be an extremely good training ground for a couple of reasons. Firstly, the diverse shows staged at The Orchard required a different marketing approach every time. It was clear that while popular, celebrity-led shows were almost always guaranteed to sell out, it was extremely difficult to get people in for more serious 'highbrow' productions, even if they were produced by well-established professional companies. Secondly, with only a limited number of local press outlets to approach for coverage, Baxter had to be increasingly creative when dealing with these journalists in order to fire their interest and get coverage. On many occasions she'd arrange photo-shoots involving her own friends and family just to give the paper a strong enough visual image under which they could mention the show.

The National Theatre

After four years, Baxter applied for a press job at the Royal National Theatre; however, it became clear that she had a different outlook on the work because of her regional theatre background. Moreover, because she had had no time to visit the National Theatre itself, her knowledge of the shows was not sufficient to land her the job. Instead, a vacancy appeared in the publications department and Baxter took that job.

Once inside the organisation, Baxter progressed through a few positions, becoming head of marketing and then co-head of development prior to taking on the full permanent position when her fellow job holder went on maternity leave. It was a progression that Baxter herself acknowledges was a result of being at the right place at the right time, as much as it was a result of her developing the right skills and seeking out opportunities. As head of development, Baxter was involved in securing funds for a US tour, taking responsibility not only for the financial side of the project but also for the general logistics surrounding the trip and a number of public appearances. 'I gained a lot of my business skills from running that tour', she comments. 'The company would turn up to a new town and there would be receptions, meetings and accommodation, all of which had to be organised in advance through phone calls from the UK.'

The National Portrait Gallery

When the job at the National Portrait Gallery fell vacant, Baxter was headhunted for the position. It was clear at this point that she was ideally suited for the post of head of press and marketing – the post encompassed both press liaison work and responsibility for securing sponsorship for events within the gallery. By now, Baxter had extensive experience in both these areas.

As her career has progressed, Baxter has received numerous training courses supplied in-house, giving her the skills she requires to do her work both within the organisation and in terms of providing an effective contact point for outside organisations to approach the gallery. She's taken courses for skills such as presentation, time management and strategic marketing. Her experience and knowledge has led to other senior positions being offered to her where she could make a significant contribution to the development of arts organisations, even if she isn't actually financially remunerated for this work. She's on the board for The Gate – a fringe theatre in London – and on the editorial board for a magazine on professional fund-raising. And while fund-raising and marketing an event can sometimes seem to be two distinct operations, Baxter sees similarities in the work: 'There are similar benefits to be had by sponsors and audiences through a specific event or production,' she says, 'you just need to sell it slightly differently.'

At the same time, her experience has shown that it is possible to switch between specific artistic areas, transferring skills from the theatre to the visual arts world. 'My job at the National Portrait Gallery is the first time I've worked in the visual arts,' she notes, 'but the industry is fairly open to you transferring from one area to another. You use the same skills, essentially, and I would say you get more scope for your career if you are open to transferring around the sector.'

Pressure

Baxter's career has included a number of significant challenges, with each new job representing a serious step up in terms of responsibilities. To some extent they have all been fairly nerve-racking positions – failure to attract sponsorship can directly result in the failure of a project in terms of finance or even impact on the contents of the arts programme itself. A failed press campaign can result in the audience staying away – which may even trigger questions over the value the organisation is giving for the public money it uses. Baxter also notes that as jobs are situated higher in the organisation, the expectations people have of you become higher and more of a challenge to meet. 'When you arrive at a new organisation you inherit your predecessor's staff and that's a challenge for you to get to know them and understand how you can work together', she says. 'At the same time, you are expected to have a great impact on the organisation as soon as you arrive – why else would you have been appointed if it wasn't to have some kind of dynamic effect?'

In general, there is very little in-house promotion in this area – simply because there are so few dedicated staff positions within artistic organisations. The Orchard Theatre, for example, had only two people working on press and publicity – a department head and their assistant. In order to get the right experience and create a career that moves forward, employees must be prepared to switch art forms, and even geographical location. And yet this mobility itself is far from straightforward, since few arts organisations share the same management structure. In other words, the marketing manager of a small visual art gallery may actually have greater responsibility over a wider area than the head of a press office at a large theatre.

For Baxter, her work has always remained creative in terms of developing effective press campaigns and attracting partners and sponsors for events, exhibitions or even capital investments. For the new wing of the National Portrait Gallery, for example, Baxter was able to involve a publicist agency in the launch. Since this company were publishers as well as publicists they could provide supporting literature alongside organising the launch itself.

Business skills

While some aspects of her work are very social – she can find herself talking to the public or to sponsors many nights, acting as the public face of the gallery – there's also a business side to the job. However, Baxter feels she has managed to get to grips with this without too much specific business training. 'You can't just be good at arts anymore,' she says, 'you need a feel for business. If you're handling budgets and resources you need those skills. But then, I control budgets and I was never any good at maths, so I think if I can do it then anyone can.' At the same time, this aspect of the job is not divorced from the context of working within the arts sector: 'The business angle is related completely to the arts world', she says. 'Everything is wrapped up with the arts, so you're always talking about something you know about and enjoy. You become aware of what can be spent on exhibitions and how much they might cost, but that doesn't stop you from appreciating and enjoying the art itself.'

Creative admin

Some areas of administration are more creative than others. Programming events in an arts venue, for example, is an extremely creative activity. This may not simply be a matter of identifying touring companies or exhibitions that should come to the venue, but of devising thematic seasons of work, creating events by bringing together diverse artists and providing a space where they can work together. It may entail offering the public a new experience, or a new perspective on the work of others. Tour management and outreach work is also immensely creative, for example bringing a piece of theatre to an audience who wouldn't usually witness this kind of work, or taking a writer on a tour of bookshops and other venues around the country. Even arranging an event such as a poetry slam, where anyone can get up and perform their own work, gives the organiser a huge creative buzz in producing an event that would not have occurred were it not for their imagination in conceiving the event and their hard work in making that idea a reality.

Other aspects of the work can be more mundane. Occasionally the work will have more in common with jobs outside the arts and media sector than with any other work inside the arts industry. Fund-raisers may still find themselves trying to balance a budget, while marketing managers may even be found stuffing envelopes for a mailshot. In general, the smaller the organisation, the more

likely it is that menial tasks will still be a feature of the administrator's work. However, even here there is the potential for
creativity at some level. Publicity managers might dream up
creative new ways to promote an event, just as an editor might
think up a new series of articles to increase the readership of their
magazine.

Job satisfaction is also to be found in effectively facilitating and
supporting the work of others – not simply by providing the
optimum conditions under which creatives can work, but
working effectively with other people within and outside the
industry. This could mean working with and managing staff who
report to you, or dealing with people from external organisations
who may want to work alongside you, creating partnerships to
your mutual benefit. The importance of skills to manage other
people in the job will depend on the size and type of the organisation, but certainly there's no way you can work in an administrative role without working with other people. Administrators
must therefore be good at organising and inspiring others, and be
expert at delegation as well as good at using their own skills.

Moving around the sector

There is a reasonable amount of employment mobility between
different art forms across the sector. A press officer working for an
art gallery can find him- or herself a new position with greater
responsibility by moving into the world of the theatre, or classical
music, and so on. To some extent, the nature of the sector necessi-
tates this. In a sector epitomised by small organisations there can
be few opportunities for in-house development and anyone
looking for promotion by waiting for their boss to move on will be
in for a long wait. Moving around the sector can be desirable for
the extra experience and new skills a different organisation can
offer. Just as one art form may influence another, the approach of a
fund-raising department in a theatre may inspire a new initiative
when brought to an art gallery.

Very often, experience gleaned from working in a regional arts
organisation can prove very valuable for someone seeking work
in a large city. Audiences in each area are completely different and
so the challenge of filling a theatre or gallery has to be met in

different ways. A regional theatre will need a wealth of new methods and initiatives to get people in. Such measures may not be necessary in the city, where the catchment area means audience numbers are naturally higher. Getting a wide range of experience will improve your ability to think laterally when approaching new problems and challenges, making you a flexible and effective worker with a lot to offer high-profile employers.

Another excellent way to use administrative skills and knowledge is in the area of funding arts organisations. Working within a regional arts office offers a great opportunity to take a wider view of the arts world, and even to concentrate on an artistic activity you are particularly interested in. Rather than working with one dedicated dance company, for example, you can address dance activities across the region. You can organise dance festivals to raise awareness of the form, act as a catalyst or be a communications channel to put practitioners in touch with each other so that they can work together and support each other.

Working in such an organisation will give you a clear insight into the process of funding productions and organisations. You will learn where the organisation's priorities exist, how applications are processed, how much funding can be found and how quickly it can be resourced. This kind of information and experience will be extremely valuable when offered to an individual arts company looking to secure funding. You might, therefore, be able to use the skills and knowledge you have gained with a regional arts office to secure a high-profile position such as head of development for an arts-based company. You may even find your level of skills means you can establish yourself as a freelance consultant to a certain sector of the arts world in the field of fund-raising.

Karen Cardy – Marketing in classical music

Karen Cardy has always been interested in classical music and has played the violin from the age of 11. Growing up in Bedfordshire she attended as many youth orchestras as possible, and while having a slightly unusual existence – she was one of only three children in her area interested in playing classical music, so found it difficult integrating the world of music with the world of school – she still had a wonderful time. She took private lessons and continued playing throughout her O and A level studies. On leaving school she took a performing arts foundation course, which enabled her to continue playing and singing. The course she took was aimed more towards community arts and she was involved with a lot of outreach work, taking music to groups of children and adults and even into prisons. She followed her foundation course with a one-year course in Newcastle in order to secure a degree in the performing arts.

In spite of this activity and obvious dedication to her instrument, Karen always knew she would not play the violin professionally. To begin with, it is generally the case that those who are going to become professional musicians have their career paths mapped out by their early teens. They have been recognised as gifted in their particular area and arrangements are made for scholarships or professional tutoring. This has to be backed by a single-minded determination to succeed with the instrument and to be willing to sacrifice everything else in order to play. While Cardy tried it for a while, she found she was unable to put in the 10 hours' practice a day that would be necessary to achieve and maintain the standard required.

Instead, she started applying for jobs in related fields. Her only direct experience of working in music at the time was when she had helped to run a contemporary music festival in Newcastle while still a student. She had fallen into this project by chance, but it had shown her that she had very good organisational skills. At the end of her degree, she decided she could benefit from getting some good vocational skills that would be valuable in the job market. She learnt to drive and took a secretarial training course – in retrospect, one of the hardest things she has ever done.

A lucky break

With these qualifications under her belt she managed to land a job at a publishers as an assistant in the sales and marketing of sheet music. While she remains mystified as to why the company employed her, it was only two weeks after she joined that her boss left the organisation, giving her the chance of immediate promotion and responsibility for running the department. She worked extensively with the sales reps and shops, gaining something of a crash course in many aspects of the music world and publishing in general.

Cardy then moved to the BBC, where she was attached to the annual Promenade Concerts, working on tie-in publications. She typeset the concert programmes and worked in a wide variety of production roles over the next few years. She was promoted within the department every three years or so, but was keen to find something new outside the department that she could get to grips with. Unfortunately, through a combination of her specialist area and the tendency for the BBC at that time to pigeonhole employees, she found herself stuck in the Proms department.

Nevertheless, Cardy made the most of the opportunities around her. She took practically every training course relevant to the music department and even took an MBA. 'I was able to apply the MBA in my job', she says. 'It helped me to understand what was going on underneath the surface of the organisation. I understood the internal organisation much better.' However, in spite of increasing her skills, the BBC remained narrow-minded in exploiting her talents. She sought satisfaction elsewhere, and while still working for the BBC she established a professional orchestra based in Luton, which she managed for three years.

Creating and running the orchestra was no mean feat. Cardy managed to fully finance and produce six concerts a year – both outdoor and indoor events at a variety of locations. Some support was even forthcoming from the local council, in spite of the low level of arts funding at the time. 'We worked to convince local businesses that we were a good investment for them in terms of sponsorship', explains Cardy. 'That kind of work can be difficult, but I found it relatively easy to go and talk to people, explaining how this would benefit them and sharing the idea as it progressed.' Finally, frustration with the BBC led her to hand in her notice, and with no particular idea of what to do next, aside perhaps from working outside the music industry altogether, she left the BBC.

The London Symphony Orchestra

When the job of marketing manager came up at the London Symphony Orchestra (LSO), Cardy was fully aware that she wasn't the ideal candidate for the job. While she had extensive experience of managing a programme of classical music and promoting this throughout the media, she had never been fully responsible for her own marketing department. In spite of this, she decided to apply and make up for lack of experience with a demonstration of her abilities.

The interview itself involved a panel of some 16 representatives from the orchestra. It was only a few minutes before her lack of experience was raised, but Cardy was well prepared. She'd carried out some research into the LSO and the classical music market they were involved in. This way, as soon as the question of experience came up she was able to present a complete marketing plan for the orchestra to the panel. She realised the positive impact she'd made when members of the panel appeared to drop the idea of questioning her and instead discussed the feasibility of the marketing plan between themselves.

Cardy was swiftly brought on board as marketing manager for the orchestra and in her first week's work she had to create some marketing material to go with the orchestra's application to the Arts Council for stabilisation funds. While this was clearly a marketing matter, Cardy at this stage didn't even know what stabilisation funds were. She worked dedicatedly on the material, day and night, and created a successful document.

The LSO is run as a collective, with each musician taking a nominal share in the company and therefore sharing in the financial gains derived from the orchestra's activities. This means, unlike orchestras where musicians may be employed on a salaried basis, they have a clear interest in furthering the activities of the orchestra and taking part in new initiatives. Karen Cardy is one of the small team of staff employed by the orchestra's managing director to run the business side of the orchestra, arranging the working lives of their musicians and making sure they all know when and where they are needed. This arrangement means that each musician is effectively self-employed and their own boss, time-tabling LSO activities alongside their own musical pursuits – which could mean playing in their own band or teaching music to others.

Hard work

For Cardy, it means there is a lot of work to do and a great deal of pressure to be effective. She's not only concerned with arranging concerts, but must ensure there will be an audience for each show. The difference between 96 per cent and 98 per cent audience attendance can be substantial once trans-lated into revenue for the orchestra. 'I always thought I worked hard for the BBC,' says Cardy, 'but it was nothing compared with this. The LSO is a young organisation with a high turnover of staff in some areas and you can burn out quite quickly. Having said that, it's a good place to come and work and I thoroughly enjoy it.'

Almost diametrically opposed to Cardy's experience at the BBC, the LSO positively encourages her to create new initia-tives that could improve the work of the orchestra or open new avenues for work. She works closely with the orchestra's managing director – a professional musician himself – and he is always keen to bring together musical quality and inno-vation with good business practice.

The image of an orchestra may be of simply playing the occasional classical concert, but the LSO is frequently booked

> for session work, whether it be for pop music, incidental TV or film soundtracks or even for advertisement jingles. And while Cardy may be dealing with arrangements in this area – arranging transport and logistics for a recording event that may occur in the next few days or weeks – she's also focused on the orchestra's activities many years in advance. If the orchestra is to go on tour nationally or internationally there are detailed arrangements to be made in terms of transport, booking venues and accommodation, as well as how the trip is to be financed.
>
> 'If you want a rewarding artistic life it's always a question of finding ways of doing that and how to earn money doing that', says Cardy. 'You need marketing skills but you still need the artistic skills to know what you're talking about.'

Moving experiences

While moving around the sector is good for gaining new experiences, skills and knowledge, to do it effectively you must have some degree of knowledge of each organisation you approach. It is no good approaching a regional theatre as box office manager, having spent time working in an art gallery, and not have any concept of what the work entails or of the priorities of your potential new employers. It seems a fairly obvious move to carry out some research into the organisation to discover the programme, the type of audience it is attracting, and so on. However, some applicants still turn up to interview with little or no idea of the type of work carried out by the company to which they are applying for work.

An open mind should be maintained within each of these roles. There is a tendency for press and publicity managers to regard arts coverage as something carried only by the broadsheet papers and specialist magazines. Ignoring the tabloid and local press is not only missing an opportunity, but can leave an organisation vulnerable to attack. In recent years, the tabloids have gone to town over a number of TV programmes, providing negative publicity sometimes prior to transmission. At the same time, the kind of furore attracted by the apparent 'mismanagement' of a publicly funded project – especially if the project has cost millions of pounds and appears to be a white elephant (eg Millennium Dome, The; 2000–2001) – can completely destroy that project. Ultimately, press and publicity managers are as much at the mercy of the press as they are able to influence the level and nature of the coverage offered. And if the public stay away as a result of bad press, or do not listen to a music act or watch a programme, it can spell disaster for the entire organisation.

These kind of roles offer the chance to work in all areas of the arts and to learn about every aspect of running an arts organisation. Press, publicity and marketing roles require an awareness of all aspects of the arts organisation. If you want to arrange an interview with the press, you need to know who would be suitable and available for that interview. In the literary world it may be possible to set up an interview with an author, providing they are not involved in rewrites or working on their next publication. Actors and theatre directors, however, are usually at their busiest in the last weeks of rehearsal – at precisely the time when the press want to feature the production. A good publicity officer will be aware of these issues and structure press contact accordingly. Equally, an effective fund-raiser should be well aware of their organisation's structure and business. It is only by having this knowledge that they can decide how much finance is required and what kind of sponsorship deals can be offered.

Helen Nattrass – Personnel management in the music industry

Until landing her first job at EMI Records, Helen Nattrass had never considered the music industry as an option for employment. Naturally, she was aware of chart music and had spent some time working in the bar scene on a casual basis, but her full-time appointment in the industry came through an employment agency who were simply advertising for someone with human resources skills to work in a 'leisure industry' company, based in West London. It was only when Nattrass was invited to interview that she discovered the company was EMI.

Originally from Liverpool, Nattrass took a degree in hospitality management at the University of Wolverhampton. She enjoyed the business aspects of the course and thoroughly enjoyed her time as a student. She worked at the Adelphi hotel in Liverpool, finding the work here very interesting. She then took a more personnel-related job as a recruitment consultant working in the West Midlands.

In some ways this work was ideal for Nattrass. She had no clear idea of what exactly she wanted to do, but working in recruitment meant she could increase her personnel skills while also staying in the loop in terms of being aware of the work opportunities that were around at the time. Eventually, a combination of frustration with the job and her partner moving to London led her to drop that job and make the move to the capital as well.

Nattrass secured a job at a central hotel in London as personnel officer. She didn't really feel she wanted to work in this sector again, but the position used her skills and knowledge while she was on the lookout for other work. Eventually that chance came through an agency who offered her a job as human resources assistant for EMI Records UK & Ireland Ltd. Clearly from this route into the sector it was not necessary for Nattrass to have any specialist knowledge of the music industry – how the business was structured or even which recording artists were signed to EMI.

Training

The job was purely administrative and at the level she entered the company could give her the training she needed to be effective in her new role. Indeed, as she progressed from assistant to human resources advisor and then to manager she was given training within the company to secure her professional qualifications with the Chartered Institute of Personnel and Development. But while she may not have needed much knowledge of the music business to secure her job, Nattrass is now well versed in the industry and uses this knowledge to facilitate the work of others in the company, both in terms of managing and developing the talent they employ and in identifying new skills that need to be brought into the company for specific projects.

The Hammersmith offices of EMI house the three record labels of the company and the support services including sales, finance, IT and legal departments. The company also still owns and manages a handful of recording studios, including Abbey Road. Once an artist has recorded their music with the A&R Manager, it is up to the people working in the record labels to develop and manage an effective marketing, press and promotion campaign that will ensure the artist reaches their maximum audience. There is no question that the company is run along business lines and that the ultimate aim is to sell product, but this does not mean that EMI's employees are purely business oriented. Ultimately, these employees feel passionately about music – about finding new talent and bringing that music to a wider audience. Indeed, they have to be passionate about their subject in order to put in the hours required, to ride out the hard times as well as enjoying the good.

Work hard, play hard

Nattrass notes that working in this industry isn't for everyone. There's a particular demand for financial and IT workers in the sector – and it is frequently these people who, firstly, do not appreciate the opportunities that exist for them in the sector, and, secondly, do not always feel at home with some of the more 'informal' aspects of the working environment. The offices here are open plan and while the culture is one of work hard, play hard, there is little in the way of strict rules governing the working day. Employees may find themselves working irregular hours in offices where there is music constantly playing and where they are expected to manage their own work rather than look to their superiors for guidance on how to achieve project targets. Some workers in the finance and IT sectors find this approach an anathema to their working life.

Nattrass herself finds the work exciting and inspiring. As a human resources manager she works with employees at all levels and in all disciplines of the company. She meets regularly with working teams – with press and marketing, for example – finding out what their next main project will be and providing personnel support to help them succeed in those projects. It may be that one of the record labels decides they want to expand into a new or different music genre and therefore needs someone with specialist skills and knowledge in that area to shape their strategy for the launch. The human resources department is proactive rather than reactive in the company, providing input at the early stages of new projects in whatever part of the company they might be.

Global opportunities

The department is also proactive in the general ongoing development of EMI's employees. With a range of internal training initiatives, the company has started to build effective succession planning into its operation, identifying possible vacancies and skill needs for the future and ensuring there will be appropriately qualified individuals ready to take those positions as and when they arise. EMI's size means it is able to develop its employees effectively and provide a varied and constantly challenging career. With offices in 70 countries, Nattrass notes the company can give individuals international assignments in order to move up the organisation. The human resources function runs an internal Web site advertising opportunities across the workforce, with the result that the majority of senior appointments are made from within the company, while most external candidates join the company at a more junior level. As testimony to this approach, it is interesting to note that the company's president joined EMI 20 years ago in the marketing department. The managing director of the EMI:Chrysalis record label has also moved through the company, working as an international product manager before becoming the marketing director of the Parlophone record label. While both these high-flying employees have been developed through the company, their careers have been driven by an unquestionable enthusiasm for music.

Nattrass admits there are some individuals who seem to think working in the music industry removes the need for them to learn about the more business-oriented skills, but there is a greater push within the company towards making employees accountable for the effectiveness of their work. People management skills are clearly of the utmost importance to success in the sector: 'To be a high-flyer you need to be a good manager and that can mean a different skill set to specific qualifications or musical knowledge', says Nattrass.

A creative business

In spite of this business-led approach it is clear that working in the industry within a company like EMI is still a creative pursuit – as is Nattrass' own work in developing and nurturing the human resources within the organisation. 'The top level managers are still being very creative for the company, but they're being creative through their employees', explains Nattrass. 'Once you get to a certain level you need to consider financial aspects, management aspects and so on. It's still hands-on and in some ways it becomes more creative than ever.'

There are only a handful of large companies within the music sector, developing, publishing and marketing popular music, although there are many smaller labels carrying out the same work in a different way. Within the industry, therefore, the opportunities for networking are extremely high and everyone within each part of the company knows everyone else who works in that function in the industry. It is therefore more than possible to build your career through sharing knowledge not only of the opportunities and challenges you might be able to take up elsewhere, but also of what might be the next big thing.

The business of art

It is clear that business skills are a necessity in many of these roles, not simply in order to run an important function in a company, but to be able to communicate effectively with external companies and organisations who may be able to offer your organisation support in some way. While there has always been a love/hate relationship between the arts and business – many an arts administrator sent on a management course has claimed that what they are being taught does not apply to their organisation since they are a 'special case' – there has been a realisation that the arts does need a more businesslike approach. This is particularly the case within organisations in receipt of public funding or targeted grants. Accountability and value for money has become paramount.

The fact is that, to some extent, artistic events can be analysed in the same way as manufacturing or service industries. There may not be a clear mechanical process to analyse, and the old argument of 'what does art do/what is the true value of art?' is still up for grabs, but the concept of a play being a product, bought by customers – the ticket-buying audience – who will only return if they get value for money, does hold water.

At the same time, administrative staff need to be aware of the possible implications of getting business involved in artistic activities. Sponsorship deals may seem lucrative but there can be difficulties with certain organisations if they are considered to be undesirable or unsuitable for association with artistic activities. An artistic organisation such as an arts venue or gallery may find they run into trouble if the artists they intend to feature do not approve of the organisations involved in funding them. Artistic activity often has a political imperative behind it; indeed, sometimes the political message can be overt and of paramount importance to the artist. This cannot be undermined through association with companies or organisations that act against that political stance.

In the media sector, the importance of business skills is unquestionable. If you are involved in the production of a magazine or newspaper, TV programme or Internet information service, it is crucial that the costs of providing that service – such as employees' pay, capital expenditure, running costs, and so on –

are met by revenues. These revenues can be the fees paid by the consumer or commissioning broadcaster, or alternatively revenues generated by advertisers who want to place their product within or next to your publication.

Lucinda Morrison – Press and publicity in the theatre

To some extent Lucinda's career path appears simple and straightforward, but what is important is the wealth of experience accumulated as she has moved from employer to employer. As she herself notes, she has always been fortunate in being in the right place with the right qualities at the right time.

She claims to have fallen into press work by accident, having originally set out to work in the editorial side of publishing. After completing an English degree she applied for an assistant's job in the editorial department of a publishers, but when it was clear that post had been filled she was offered a job in the publicity department. 'Working there was a revelation', she says. 'I think most people in the industry start at the very bottom and you do spend a lot of time photocopying, but I had a very supportive boss who gave me lots of projects to do.'

The publishers where Morrison worked were a fairly large company, which meant she could take full advantage of working across the range of publications being produced and promoted. One day she might find herself working on a textbook about child abuse, creating press releases for distribution to broadsheet newspapers or special interest publications. The next day she could be working on a romantic novel for the more popular reader market. This also meant she had contacts across a wide range of the media – newspaper editors and journalists of all kinds – rather than simply book reviewers. This range of contacts is something she no longer has in the theatre, since she now deals exclusively with arts journalists. While she has a closer relationship with these people than she did with her previous contacts, she does occasionally miss the variety of that work.

Having stayed in publishing for four or five years, slowly moving up the ranks within the publicity department, Morrison decided she wanted to move into the area of theatre. She took some time off travelling and then returned to the job market but was unable to find any suitable vacancies. She returned to the publishing world, but was there for only six months when a job became vacant at the Chichester Festival Theatre. The theatre gave Morrison a great deal of useful experience, since it had a good enough reputation to attract the national press as well as enjoying strong local press contacts. It also tended to farm out the more mundane tasks such as direct mailing to external companies. Morrison was able to enjoy a working environment that did not require extremely hard work to raise press interest, but was also not so high profile that she was under a great deal of pressure.

The National Theatre

About four years later Morrison moved on, this time to work with a well-known PR agency in London. The agency dealt with a number of West End shows, but also featured TV work, providing insight into another area of the media for Morrison. Working at this agency brought her into contact with the National Theatre on many occasions and so when the post of senior press officer came up she was ideally placed to make a successful application. Three years later she was promoted to head of the press office.

'I was reluctant to take the job of head of the press office at first because I love the theatre and so working hands-on was very important to me', she says. 'Once you become head of the department your job becomes more to do with managing a team of staff to deal with the practical issues day to day.' However, Morrison has found her top job still to be creative and enjoyable and certainly she has no plans to move to anywhere else in the foreseeable future.

'The thing about publicity in this theatre is that you never know what's going to come up', she says. 'You know how certain projects are going to be organised around which productions but you still don't know if you're going to get the press on board or how they're going to approach you or who might be on the end of the phone.' Indeed, working for such a high-profile company as the National can be something of a double-edged sword. On the one hand the theatre is practically guaranteed to attract press interest whether it is to do with the appointment of a new director, the announcement of a new season or the opening night of a new production. At the same time, however, any negative aspects of the theatre will be pounced on, requiring action on the part of the press team to answer queries and provide a response.

Lateral thinking

Morrison particularly enjoys projects that require a degree of lateral thought in promoting rather than straightforward interviews with actors and directors. A play might feature a portrayal of an actor, for example, leading Morrison to put together a package that suggests an article about the portrayal of actors on stage in other shows. Since journalists are constantly bombarded by all manner of press releases and information about new shows, Morrison believes it is necessary to put together something more detailed – a full article suggestion – rather than simply telling them what's on, who's in it and when it's on.

Satisfying the demand for celebrity interviews is another aspect of Morrison's work. While the press may be keen to interview actors, actresses and directors in the run-up to the opening night, this is precisely the time when these people are at their busiest, concentrating on rehearsals and putting together the show. The press officer must be as sensitive to their needs as they are dedicated to giving a good story to the journalists. The rise in interest in celebrity actors and actresses has made this part of the job more of a challenge, since many performers shy away from publicity because of the invasion of privacy it can sometimes entail.

'When you're dealing with publicity for a book, the author could have finished work on it years before it is published,' notes Morrison, 'so it's relatively easy to organise interviews and even public appearances for them around the country. Here, the main publicity comes during the last two weeks of rehearsal. In addition, there's no contractual obligation for actors to do publicity for the show, so you have to find things they are happy and able to do.' Other parts of the National's work are more difficult to promote. The theatre runs an extensive education programme, but very few journalists will express an interest in this area unless the initiative is led by a big name.

The Web presence

The Internet has produced new challenges in Morrison's work. On the one hand the World Wide Web offers a new arena in which to communicate the activities of the theatre to a wider audience. The use of the National's Web pages is still being evolved and there is the potential to post video and audio clips of current or past productions on the site to promote the theatre further. Realising this will, however, require new negotiations over remuneration for writers, performers and those connected with creating the productions.

Another problem created by the Internet is the proliferation of companies applying for press tickets from the theatre. Countless theatre-oriented Web sites have contacted the theatre asking for complimentary tickets in exchange for a review to be posted on their site. As Morrison points out, they have to be extremely careful in granting these requests, ensuring that the site is professionally managed and used regularly by people who are potential audience for the theatre. Without this assurance, not only can the press department end up issuing press tickets without receiving anything in return, but the profile of the theatre itself can be compromised by appearing on a poor-quality site.

Getting to the top and staying there

With dedication and by building a good track record it is possible to arrive at a high-profile position such as head of press and publicity for an arts organisation in a relatively short space of time. High flyers may gain such seniority by the time they are in their early 30s, riding high on their ability to produce effective campaigns at the drop of a hat, a result of youthful enthusiasm as much as clear skills in this area. Two problems may then arise: first, the problem of burnout, and second, the fact that there isn't really anywhere else for that employee to go.

Burnout is a big problem in the arts sector, especially in smaller organisations where administrators may be carrying out a myriad of tasks for the company. It can be difficult to constantly generate new ideas or even to master yet more enthusiasm for events that simply mean you're working long hours away from home and still have to deal with limited or dwindling financial and logistical resources. If you do find yourself in this position you must find new ways of inspiring yourself. This could mean going on a training course or taking a break to study something completely different. Many magazine editors take refresher courses in areas of journalistic skills simply to keep in touch with the daily business of creating copy. These courses help them to keep a fresh outlook on their work and their publication.

If you do find yourself on the top rung of your organisation with nowhere else to progress, further challenges may still exist in the other parts of the arts sector – in larger organisations or perhaps a completely different area of the arts. At the same time it should be noted that some workers do reach a certain point in their career and decide to leave the arts industry altogether. Having enjoyed some major achievements in this field they need to find an entirely new career to reinvigorate their working life.

Sue Rose – Publicity at a major arts venue

Sue Rose's career in the arts industry has really shadowed the growth of media coverage of the arts. Not only did she work on one of the first publications to feature listings information, she also established press offices and PR strategies for a number of arts organisations, including the Arts Council itself. With a strong background in journalism, she firmly believes that it is necessary to understand the machinations of the press, the demands of arts journalists and the pressures they are under from day to day in order to effectively provide information to them and to secure good coverage for any artistic event.

Rose's early days followed the established route for journalists at the time. She took extensive secretarial training, which gave her good shorthand and typing skills, and then started out as a trainee on a regional paper. Rather than undergoing any formal training, she simply picked up the skills she required as she went along. Working for the *Yorkshire Evening Post* she was responsible for a number of different parts of the paper, eventually including a women's interest page. She was moved to the London offices of the paper when her husband was moved to the capital and worked as a general reporter there. She found her work was moving increasingly towards arts-related stories – even if they only consisted of 'Yorkshire Actor Made Good' type features. While working for the *Post* she started a column detailing events that were happening over the weekend. This became a listings column – a concept that has since grown to make up a significant sector of media output in itself.

Finding the hours and demands of journalism incompatible with looking after a young family, Rose moved to work on the PR side of the arts world. She took a job at the press office of Christie's auctioneers and for seven years worked at promoting sales and events taking place at the auction house.

The Arts Council years

From there she moved to the Arts Council to set up its first press office in 1978. From small beginnings, Rose was able to have a great impact on the promotion of the arts, forging alliances with arts boards and other arts organisations across the UK. When she first arrived, the Arts Council was attracting more than its fair share of bad press, principally because whenever funding had to be cut – whether to an orchestra, theatre or to the regions – the Arts Council would be fiercely criticised by the arts organisations affected and take all of the blame. In fact, it was not the Arts Council who were the real culprits. They had no control over the actual level of funding, they simply decided where the cuts should fall. Sue Rose worked to bring together arts organisations to campaign for sustained funding for the arts, thereby making it a concerted and focused effort by the arts world, rather than allowing separate organisations to undermine each other or pass the blame.

Other initiatives sought to promote the profile of the arts across the media. Recognising the effectiveness of lobby groups in industry and education, Rose established a similar lobby group for the arts which would comment on and promote specific issues within the arts world. Having gone from a position where there were only three arts correspondents in Fleet Street, soon every media organisation had appointed its own dedicated correspondent. Monthly briefings were established between the lobby group and the correspondents, again improving relationships between the arts organisations and the press, and guaranteeing that the arts would receive serious and considered coverage that extended beyond press releases concerned with specific performances.

Rose was also able to work closely with the arts boards, encouraging them to establish their own press offices to promote artistic activities and achievements in their own catchment area. She even helped to establish an arts journalism award, thereby giving this area of journalism recognition equal to that of any other news.

Going freelance

With two years left before retirement, Rose decided to take early retirement from the Arts Council. However, rather than putting her feet up and going to coffee mornings, she went freelance in the field of PR. She worked for many organisations, including the Royal Festival Hall. She was involved with education projects at the London Symphony Orchestra and continued to work in the field of media relations training – another area of work she had developed while at the Arts Council. This training included coaching senior people within arts organisations on how to communicate with the press and how to present themselves when being interviewed or during public functions.

At this time the head of the press office at the Royal Festival Hall left and while they were searching for a replacement, Rose was invited to fill the gap. She took the post at two days a week and while she continued her media training activities, she stopped her other PR work simply because it created a conflict of interest. Of course, the post at the Royal Festival Hall expanded, as these things have a tendency to do, and soon Rose was working three days a week. She offered to help recruit a replacement, but in the end took the post herself for a year, maintaining that she would still not do this as a full-time job. She's still there now, but has time to do other work, including running the occasional training course.

'All too few PR people in the arts have worked in the press and therefore they do not understand the pressures on journalists or people working in TV', she says. 'I think you need to know that because otherwise you're just acting as an information service, which is not what you should be.' While Rose made her move into PR in order to escape the pressure of deadlines and the irregular hours of the work, she has not totally escaped these in her current post. She realises that journalists work round the clock, trying to find stories and to hit deadlines. They will still be working bank holidays and weekends and therefore while she may not be needed in the office, she does need to be contactable.

Her work at the Arts Council required a knowledge of the political side of the arts – where government funding was coming from and how that funding was managed and would be managed in the future. Rose admits that such an awareness is not necessary for people working in other areas of the arts or for organisations operating further away from the funding front-line, but this is another area of knowledge that has given her attractive skills for arts organisations.

A plethora of paths

Rose is amazed that there is still no single clear path into working in the sector, but believes that the best way to secure success is to get into an organisation and get down to work. It may mean months of drudgery but there is no better way to understand the day-to-day work of the organisation or to learn how to communicate with the media. At the same time, she notes, just because you rise through the organisation and gain greater standing, you should never expect to avoid mundane work. Even as head of the press office at the Royal Festival Hall, she still finds herself photocopying material and stuffing envelopes. Rose also believes it is valuable for employees in this area to have taken a degree course in something unrelated to the arts, and then to take a vocational course on journalistic skills in order to get into the industry. General arts and media degrees are simply too commonplace to offer any specific attraction to employers.

'You have to start a career of this type at the ground floor', says Rose. 'Use your eyes and ears, do the dull jobs and look for the opportunities. Preferably you should be in a large organisation where you can learn things from other people rather than in a small one where you have to do everything with no direction from anyone else.' While it is impossible to ensure everyone can get a position like this, Rose also notes that those who find themselves in smaller organisations can turn to their regional arts organisations to provide resources for training and coaching programmes.

Production roles

As mentioned above, some roles from the media industry have been included under the title of administrators for the sake of structuring this book rather than because they are pure admin jobs. Many of them would be better described as production roles rather than administration, but they are similarly placed between the original artist (the presenter on TV and radio, the journalist in print media) and the media itself (the TV production company or the publishing company). Again, these people may not be concerned with the strategic direction of their employing organisations and they may not have a direct input on content, but they do play a crucial role in managing the quality of output from an organisation.

Being the editor of a publication, whether in print or online on the Internet, can mean different things according to the individual publication. It is still a reasonably hands-on occupation, although in general you will find yourself working with material delivered by other writers and contributors, rather than generating it yourself. Some editors may be involved in the commissioning process, determining the content of a publication and finding journalists ready and willing to provide that content. They may also need to assess offers of content made by journalists who want to contribute to the magazine. They may have a team of staff reporters who they need to direct and manage to ensure specific stories are covered.

In smaller publications, the editor may still create content. This is particularly the case for Internet publications where the use of technology has effectively done away with other levels of publishing employees. There is no need for production editors or sub-editors to check and lay out the text when one person can create the text, check it for spelling and grammar and post it directly to the Web site. This has become more common as the potential of the Internet as an immediate information source has been realised.

Editors may also take on an ambassadorial role for their publication. Nowadays it is not sufficient to rely on good content to attract readers and establish a publication's reputation, one must be proactive, taking the publication to the readers and raising awareness of its existence. This role could mean public speaking, meeting important people within the sector you are writing for, or cultivating a public, and even celebrity, image. A publication's popularity can be increased if the editor is a known pundit and someone whose opinion is sought by other parts of the media – for example, a broadcast news programme turning to the political editor of *The Times* for their opinion on a certain news story.

Circulation wars

In the print media, circulation figures have a direct impact on the amount of revenue achievable through advertising sales. Advertisers will pay more money, the more valuable they consider the paper to be. If you can guarantee to place an advert in front of a target audience, you can charge more for that advertising space. The same applies to commercial radio and TV reporting – attract more viewers or listeners and you'll have increasing advertising revenues. The editor must therefore direct the publication to be attractive to readers and to advertisers. Doing this means hitting the right balance of the commercial and the innovative – providing readers with what they want as well as what you think they should know about. It may seem attractive to offer a popular information service, or one that directly reflects the concerns and ideas of certain advertisers, but this could be at the cost of providing an independent and reliable news service. To be a successful editor you need to find the right balance and have the determination and belief to stick to your approach, carving out a clearly identifiable information service that will not be compromised by pandering to current tastes or the expectations of the advertising department.

John Sage – Executive editor in new media

John Sage's rise through the media has coincided with the increase in information channels and technology-driven platforms across which news and information can be transmitted. Having started his career in the traditional way, taking a trainee reporter position on the Brighton _Evening Argus_, he attended journalism training school, gaining the crucial basic skills that would prove relevant at every step of his career.

Once he had completed the course, he returned to the _Argus_ and worked dedicatedly on the paper, rising through the ranks to the post of senior reporter. Like many others who have worked on the local press, he found the combination of deadlines plus the incredible variety of stories, features and articles he could work on provided him with extensive and very satisfying experience. He was promoted to the position of news editor in his early 20s – a relatively young age to be in charge of a newsroom, particularly since the _Argus_ itself had a good reputation within the industry as a quality regional paper. He notes that the paper gave him the support he needed to make this move and he was able to benefit fully from this incredible learning experience.

From local to national

After a couple of years, he moved out of Brighton, out of local journalism and into national journalism. Again, this progression is not unusual. At some point, local and regional journalists must make a definite decision as to where they want their career to lead. They can choose to stay in the regional press, rising through the management hierarchy to become chief editor of the publication, or perhaps to oversee a number of local publications according to the size of the publishing company and the opportunities that exist. There is also the option of moving into more specialist press areas such as consumer publications or the business press. Sage decided, however, that having proven his worth at the _Argus_ he would work in the national press.

He first joined a news agency called UK News. This organisation was a general news source for the national press. However, following the loss of a major contract, serious cutbacks left Sage without a job. He worked briefly with PA News as a reporter before joining Teletext in the summer of

1996 as deputy editor. He joined the company at the point when the information services provided were at the start of a huge expansion. When Sage joined, the company had simply been supplying text services to ITV and Channel 4. Their service was operating in direct competition with the BBC – who were in fact their only competitor. Over the next few years new services were created by Teletext for Internet users, digital TV channels and WAP (Wireless Application Protocol) technology.

Training

Teletext promoted Sage through the ranks, providing relevant training courses along the way. He moved to assistant editor and after spending six months as acting editor-in-chief he secured the position on a permanent basis in spring 2000. As he has become more senior, he has found his remit expanding, so that today he is responsible for the service delivered not only on terrestrial TV, but across every media the company uses.

Training provision has supported John at every step of his promotion and has become increasingly management oriented rather than addressing purely practical skills. That said, he has still taken the occasional session on sub-editing or refresher courses in law along the way, ensuring that his professional skills do not go stale. In his current position he has also had training in public relations so that he could be a good figurehead and spokesperson for the service. 'I think each stage has been a combination of receiving training and learning on the job', says Sage. 'Certainly as I've moved into new media there's an awful lot of knowledge you need to absorb. But if I went away on a course for every new technology I'm working with I'd never be in work.'

With live electronic news platforms operating 24 hours a day, Teletext's service quality relies on its being up to date and accurate in its reporting. The TV-based service alone is updated some 100,000 times a day, a concept that is far removed from the deadlines and working timetable of a regional or national daily newspaper. 'You still have the same peaks and troughs as you get with any part of the media – TV or newsprint,' says Sage, 'but there's a great deal of pressure on our journalists to produce accurate and compelling content in a live environment, which is a pressure their peers elsewhere do not have.'

Keeping up to date with technology

Indeed, news-gathering and journalism is really only half of the equation in Sage's job. To ensure the company remains at the forefront of information services he must find and develop new services to meet the expanding electronic platforms in the marketplace. The service delivered must be appealing to the user – a question of presentation as well as quality of content. 'Electronic journalism needs wider skills than those associated with the traditional press', says Sage. 'You might not need to understand how to program something or how exactly the technology works, but you do need to be aware of the possibilities and able to work with people who understand it better than you. Editors in this area need to understand what the technology can do as well as being good journalists and able to spot a good story.'

Sage claims he does miss the straightforward journalistic work that has decreased as his managerial responsibilities have increased. 'I think every journalist remains a journalist at heart and struggles with the idea of being a professional manager', he says. However, for every element of his former work that he has given up, he has found some new issue or area of interest to motivate and inspire him. He still chairs the daily editorial conference at which content issues are discussed whenever he can, just to keep his hand in on the practical side. 'My current job has a mix of creativity and management work', notes Sage. 'But it's being creative in the sense of seeing where the company's going to go and making sure the output reflects that direction.'

Content is king

According to Sage, basic journalism skills are still in high demand across the new media sector and especially within Internet-based companies. He notes that the past few years have demonstrated that while Internet retail has had mixed fortunes, sites with good content enjoy a greater degree of success. 'Get the basics first and use those skills until you know you can handle your chosen area with confidence', he advises. 'If you move too fast, you can find yourself in an area you're not confident with.'

Alongside this, Sage believes journalists who are able to become specialists within a certain field of interest may have a slight advantage in the jobs market compared with those who can offer only generalist skills: 'The fact is that in years to come people will not use only one information source in preference to another, but they will take different sources according to the information they require', he explains. 'Specialists will be able to offer their knowledge and services directly to that audience rather than the users having to go through a huge monolithic service.'

To some extent this is already happening as Internet users can use bookmarks or online services to construct their own newspapers, channelling information from a variety of sites. The specialist journalist will certainly have great success if they can establish themselves as the highest quality supplier of specific information. 'At the end of the day, knowledge is crucial,' says Sage, 'because in a world where people are being bombarded with information they will go to the source they trust. If by refining your specialist skills you become a trusted information source you will be very valuable in the future.'

Freelance operations

While administrative-type roles within the arts and print media usually mean full-time contracts with single employers, corresponding roles in TV and film production – such as producer, editor and director – are usually run on short-term contracts or a freelance basis. This means high-flyers in this area will work for a variety of employers across a range of programmes, changing contracts and jobs every few months.

This immediately brings new pressures to these workers. Not only must they deliver a high standard of work for the projects on which they work, but they must also ensure they have a good network of contacts to provide a constant source of work for them within the industry. They need to run themselves as if they were a small business – effectively publicising their own skills and managing their own finances rather than simply taking a pay cheque each month. These workers need the skills of the creatives as well as the methodical approach of the administrative workers. As a reflection of their working conditions, these workers may attract a higher weekly wage than their full-time employed counterparts.

Job roles

Producers work across all types of broadcast media. It is their responsibility to bring together the elements needed for a programme and to ensure that the show happens as and when required. They will determine the staff and technical resources required for a show and be responsible for budgeting the entire project – including everything from performer and crew fees through to the cost of hospitality services. Of course, the job will be different according to the media concerned. Bringing together a live radio programme is a completely different ball game to coordinating a feature film, which is a completely different ball game to producing a pre-recorded TV show.

The director of a film or TV programme is responsible for the look of the show as it appears on screen. It is their responsibility to bring out the best performances from the cast or presenters, and by working with the technical staff to ensure the final product looks and sounds good. The director of a TV drama or film will often work with the writer on the film script itself. The amount of input and influence a director has on a final feature film can be seen from the way in which films are described as being 'by' the director, rather than the writer or anyone else.

The editor, meanwhile has a technical and artistic role. Working alongside the director, it is the editor's job to create the final film through selecting and bringing together the best parts of recorded material – be it film or video footage. The editor may also be responsible for integrating the soundtrack with the visuals of a programme and ensuring, especially in TV, that the programme does what it is meant to do within its time constraints and the demands of the slot it is filling.

The key to success in all these areas is to build up experience, to deliver good-quality programmes and to ensure you are known within the industry. It is rare – and indeed practically impossible – for producers or editors to go straight to the top of their profession, no matter how skilled they may be. It is absolutely necessary to start at the bottom and slowly build up the knowledge and contacts required.

Jeremy Mills, TV director

By the age of 10, Jeremy Mills had decided he wanted to be a TV director. He had no immediate friends or family in the arts or media world, but nonetheless developed a passion for this area. This passion has driven his career from working as a sound recordist through to his current position as one of the three co-directors of Lion TV, an independent company that provides many hours of programming to terrestrial and non-terrestrial channels, including new media, throughout the world.

Mills' first step along his career path came while he was still at school when he teamed up with a friend who was involved in sound recording. Mills followed this friend around his local area recording all sorts of events – from brass bands to choirs to pop groups. Through this work he developed a contact with the local BBC radio station in Plymouth and started going there in his spare time to watch the work they carried out and help out however he could.

At the time the local BBC stations played a greater role in creating output than they do today. They were effectively run along the lines of today's Radio 4, creating high-quality packages and diverse programmes across a large geographical catchment area. At the age of 14, Mills was spending weekends and holidays at the station, gradually learning about the business and finding more projects to which he could contribute: 'The studio managers realised because I was passionate about the work they could leave me to get on with it', notes Mills. 'In the end they'd go off to the bar and leave me to do any recording and editing that was needed for their show.' At the age of 16, Mills received his first BBC pay cheque.

BBC Plymouth ran TV studios alongside the radio station, so whenever the opportunity arose, Mills would shadow the directors here, watching them working in the role he had set his heart on. The TV studio produced a wide range of output – from concerts to dramas, documentaries and news – and again, Mills watched the floor managers and studio staff working together to create this output. While his principal function at the station was still making tea and coffee, Mills was already getting a kick out of the 'train set' quality he saw in controlling and coordinating each part of the production in order to create a successful programme.

A degree of success

University did nothing to stop Mills' progression. Finding himself in Bristol he simply started working at the BBC studios there. At 19 he was working on programmes as a floor manager and a year later he was offered a job at BBC Plymouth, resulting in him dropping out of college in favour of getting down to doing the job itself. It's a move he believes was absolutely the right thing for him to do at the time, although in retrospect he wonders if he should have completed his degree course.

Working seven days a week as a studio manager, Mills still used his free time to learn about broadcasting and to push himself in the direction he wanted to go. He worked shifts on the radio from 5.30 am to 2 pm and then stayed on in his own time, shadowing the work of the directors for another five hours. 'Basically I kept nagging them to let me do something on a programme', says Mills. 'At first they let me direct a short insert for one of the shows and having done that I would nag for something more complicated and so on.' Again, the range of shows produced by the studios gave Mills a wide range of experience. There were magazine shows, concerts and even the occasional studio-based drama, each of which demanded new skills and offered a different learning experience.

Working live

Soon Mills transferred to London, where he worked within the news department of the BBC. This was a slight change in the type of programming he was used to but he enjoyed this part of the work because while there was a lot of preparation to do before the show, it was broadcast live, so once it was over the staff could simply wipe the slate clean ready for the next day. Any mistakes or mishaps that happened along the way had to be dealt with as they occurred, but at the end of the day you could walk away from the show knowing you'd done your best.

Mills finally became a director when he worked for the *Food and Drink Programme* at the BBC. He worked on the programme for a couple of years, picking up a number of other film and documentary projects along the way. He then directed *The Vet*, his first series for the BBC, followed by a similarly formatted documentary called *The Doctor*. Having established himself in this area of the BBC's output, he took more senior roles in the documentary department, becoming executive producer for *Children's Hospital* and the *Airport* series of programmes.

'When I moved on to producing I was afraid I would miss the more creative side of the work', admits Mills. 'But then again, *Children's Hospital* was a massive 20-part series, so I had to be creative in a different way in order to get the programme together.' This creativity manifested itself in Mills' approach to assembling the production team – the directors, editors and programme producers who would do the day-to-day work. 'You can also be creative in terms of the place where you're setting the programme, and the stories you try to tell', Mills notes.

Independence day

Within the BBC the only opportunity open to Mills now was to move into senior management – to take on a role that would be more strategic and less about influencing or creating the output itself. Mills resisted this and at the same time decided to get away from the constraints of working purely for the BBC documentary department. At the time not only was the old structure of the BBC altering, but there were all sorts of programme ideas Mills wanted to pursue that would be difficult to develop within the corporation itself. As a result he co-founded an independent production company with a couple of like-minded colleagues who also had been working for the BBC.

'We wanted to make more diverse programmes', explains Mills. 'In BBC documentaries if you came up with an idea for a quiz show or whatever, it would be impossible to get that idea off the ground. You were viewed as more of a traitor than if you'd gone to work for Channel 4.'

Lion TV were at the forefront of the 'docu-soap' format – the TV programme that combines the informative approach of a documentary with character-driven story lines. Much copied and finally loathed by critics simply because every other new programme commissioned appeared to be a docu-soap, the genre was indicative of another trend within TV programme-making where programme types could be cross-fertilised to evolve new forms of entertainment.

New media

Lion are also working in the area of new media, creating material for Web broadcast, sometimes as tie-ins with their own programming output, sometimes as stand-alone projects. In spite of these new and expanding markets, Mills maintains that the approach to creating good material is, in essence, the same as it always has been: 'Our idea behind the whole area of new media is that with all of this – film, TV, Internet – ultimately it's all about story-telling. Audiences do not pick up on ideas or genres or broadcast media alone, it's the content that attracts them. Whether you're creating a news item or putting together a film you have to engage the audience with that story.'

Looking back over his career so far, Mills admits the restructuring of the BBC means it is unlikely that anyone can gain the same wealth of experience in programme-making as he was able to access as he grew up. However, he believes it is still possible to get important experience by working with any TV company and demonstrating that you have the drive and passion to learn and progress. Rather than studying and intellectualising the process of programme-making, he learnt by watching and by doing – relying on his intuition for editing decisions rather than because theoretically it was the right thing to do. 'At the end of the day I think you have to try these things out and see what happens', he says. 'If you want to make films or TV shows, then experiment as wildly and madly as possible. Don't just try and emulate what you see, you'll spend a lot of time in your career creating what other people want – but if you get the chance, experiment and come up with something exciting and different.'

Going in at the top

While many TV and film directors grow their careers in a similar way, there is a place for the maverick, first-time director and film maker who is determined to break the rules and create their film no matter what. Over the past few years it has been clear that success in the film industry does not require big budgets, lots of technical equipment or expensive special effects. *The Blair Witch*

Project stands as a great example of low-budget film making – shot on hand-held video cameras, the film proved a popular success, as well as impressing critics and the film industry alike.

The Internet is already providing a new showcase platform for directors and film-making talent and its use will grow as bandwidth issues are resolved and computers can exchange information at a quicker rate. With the availability and ease of use of digital cameras it is now relatively inexpensive to produce a good-quality video-based product that can be played back on any personal computer with multimedia software.

Creating your own film and finding the right channels through which to publicise it can result in high profiles for directors, producers and editors alike, but unless the film is an out and out hit, it is unlikely to result in much financial gain or even new work. If the film is successful, there may be someone out there who will offer to finance the next movie, but will you be able to deliver something of that quality again? In some cases the reason why these productions enjoy success is because the low budget on which they were created inspired innovative camera work or served to highlight the quality of the story and script. As soon as money enters the equation the director gets distracted by considerations such as the great cast they can employ and the special effects within their grasp. As a result, the successful aspects of the original production fall by the wayside. To put it simply, going into the industry at the top may well be an attractive proposition, but it brings with it an increased risk of failure. As soon as you've scaled the dizzy heights of screen success you are likely to be turned over in the search for the next big thing. So how can you increase your chances of getting highly paid work over the long term?

This is where a strong background in the industry becomes important. If you have demonstrable skills and knowledge relevant to the industry, then you will have obvious value to the industry outside the hype surrounding your success. Having a strong background and experience in directing different sorts of programmes or understanding absolutely how other programmes and films are made means other companies are likely to offer you work and bring you into future projects rather than shying away from you as a maverick who can only deliver on his or her own projects.

In TV you may successfully work on an innovative programme format. You might create the next *Weakest Link* quiz show or devise another spin on *Big Brother* – but the majority of the time the work available will be run-of-the-mill, prime-time fodder. Unless you have the right skills to work on these kinds of programmes and to produce precisely what the production company have agreed, your high-flying credentials as an innovative and ground-breaking director, producer or editor could count for nothing.

Jane King – Managing editor in print

Having spent a little over 20 years working in the print media, Jane King is now managing editor of five human resources related titles at Reed Business Information. Reed is a large company of around 2,000 employees, publishing titles directed at the business market, covering sectors from computing to medical practice. King's career effectively splits into two parts: her training and early development in the local press, followed by her recruitment and subsequent promotion through Reed.

King went straight from school to being a cub reporter at a local paper, receiving immediate news-gathering and writing experience, covering local events, weddings and anything else considered half newsworthy. She learnt her basic skills on the job, watching her copy being criticised and ripped up by the paper's sub-editors. The paper put her through three years of training under a National Council for the Training of Journalists (NCTJ) apprenticeship scheme. Even at this level, with a heavy workload, deadline pressure and exhaustive hours she found the work immensely enjoyable and stimulating. She was driven by a general news agenda, so was able to cover any subject that came up, rather than specialising in any area or section of the newspaper.

Trade press

Having taken a career break to go travelling, she was lured to the offices of Reed Business Information, and was appointed deputy news editor of a magazine aimed at the retail sector. The move to the trade press was not simply taken because of the increase in salary the position offered, but also because of the career opportunities available within Reed. At the time, the trade press was regarded with a degree of disdain – as if journalists were selling their souls by working in this sector. Today, however, King believes trade and business publications are acknowledged as playing an important part within the media industry. She believes it's a harder kind of publication to get right in terms of editorial style and content, but that it also has the potential for a creative approach. Every publication should enjoy a high profile and be well respected within the interest community it serves.

Continuing her eclectic approach to journalistic subjects, King worked across a variety of publications in about 10 different positions, moving steadily up the editorial ladder and into management. She's written about Mars Bars for publications aimed at newsagents and about social care issues for doctors and nurses. At each publication she tended to work as deputy editor before taking the top editorial position and then moving on to the next new challenge. In her current section – human resources publications – she has moved from editor of one magazine to group editor and finally to managing editor for all the titles within the department.

Alongside this variety of work, Reed have provided her with extensive training. This has principally been focused in the management area, providing her with the skills required at each new level of employment. Part of the training has developed her skills for internal management – organising people, motivating teams, and so on. At the same time, her PR and public speaking skills have also been developed to help her promote the titles she works on within the industry readership groups. After all these years she is still keen to learn new skills and keep ahead of the game – constantly learning new techniques to help her cope with the ever-increasing workload.

The long-term view

In her current position, King is basically dealing with publishing management. She is responsible for taking a strategic approach across the titles – deciding where the publications should be in three to five years time and then ensuring the editorial team work to realise that target. When she first came to *Personnel Today*, the leading magazine within the department, she found the publication to be a little lacklustre in the marketplace. It was certainly a good-quality read but it did not enjoy much of a profile within the profession and was following and reporting on trends rather than pre-empting them or setting the agenda. By taking the publication to a weekly format, creating and managing a new editorial team and enhancing contacts between the publication and leading practitioners in the human resources field, it has been possible to move the publication forward, increasing the readership and turning it into a market leader.

'You do have to make the decision at some stage of your career as to whether you want to continue writing or whether you want to move into management and take a different role', says King. 'That decision depends on asking yourself what you enjoy doing and what it is about your skills that you are good at. Not everyone wants to take on editorial work', she notes. Indeed, King has seen some examples of competent journalists being promoted into management positions that have simply not suited their talents. 'You can be absolutely useless at spotting the best stories and still be an excellent manager', she says. 'If you have commercial sense and can give the impression of moving a publication in a specific direction it doesn't matter. The days when an editor in the business press had to be a superb writer with a sharp eye for the subject are over.'

Thanks to her longevity at Reed, King has found herself gradually co-opted on to sundry boards and panels responsible for other aspects of company practice. She works with other senior managers improving the way in which knowledge is shared across the organisation. She also has some influence over staffing and salary matters for the journalists they employ. Again, these responsibilities pull her more in a management direction than anything directly related to journalistic practice.

Keeping hands-on

At the same time, she still finds time to provide input on the magazines themselves. She will scrutinise leading stories and bylines, offering useful advice on the magazines as they go out. She had recently agreed to write up a particular news story for one publication but her other responsibilities prevented her from delivering copy.

It's hardly surprising that she found herself unable to complete this last purely journalistic task. It's a considerable challenge to keep pace with the information that comes to her desk on a daily basis. King receives around 80 e-mails per day that must be dealt with, a third of which may have important repercussions for one or all of the magazines. Now the titles have achieved a good profile in the human resources sector, research companies and other organisations frequently seek out a magazine to offer joint ventures in projects or exclusive access to reports and research programmes. King must analyse these offers and decide whether or not they are worthwhile for the magazine. It is a decision that she must make quickly and effectively, since the potential partner will be keen to find an alternative publication if they are not interested.

It is King's responsibility to manage the future direction of the titles and this includes taking the titles onto the Internet, a task that has already raised a number of questions to do with content and editorial control within the office. Ultimately, King believes the *Personnel Today* print title and the Web-published title will have to work in direct competition with one another, tracking down their own exclusive stories and remaining independent of each other in terms of content and style. However, at this stage the Web page and the paper are produced by the same team of journalists, with the result that the Web editor and paper editor find themselves in contention over which media should break which story.

The challenges of new media

Naturally, with a background in newsprint journalism, King, like many others in her profession, is faced with the challenge of understanding the potential of the new media and finding ways to exploit the possibilities. While some reporters and editors with Reed – and indeed within her section – are at ease with the Net, since they use it on a regular basis in order to track down stories and contacts, there is generally a lack of technical knowledge within the organisation, which can leave the journalist team frustrated and at the mercy of IT staff when things go drastically wrong. At least with the print side of the operation, everyone knows how to correct errors.

Other differences between managing the Web and paper publications will be reflected in the editorial content of each. Not only does the Internet demand instant updating whenever stories break or develop, but it recognises no geographical barrier. Therefore, any material published must be written to appeal to a potential worldwide audience. King admits that since she is already under pressure to work with the editors of the other publications, she has little time to spend getting up to speed on the Internet. 'Probably in three years time all my work will be dedicated to delivering information via technology rather than managing paper', she says. But for the moment, certainly, King is not about to make the switch to a paperless office.

New stories

At the heart of all these roles in the media, as with the majority of creative roles, is the ability to tell a story. That story can be anything – it can be the subject of a documentary, it can be a fictional tale told in cartoon form, it can be a news report. Magazine editors, TV producers and film directors have to be able to focus on the story they are putting across and ensure that it is communicated to the audience in the best way possible. Stories draw audiences into books, newspapers and Web sites. They make people go to the cinema and the theatre. You can be as technically clever as you like but unless that technical wizardry serves the storytelling process it will be a waste of time.

The most challenging aspect in all these areas of work – from the fund-raiser to the producer, the director to the tour manager – is that as an employee your reputation is usually only regarded to be as good as the last project you completed. Produce an excellent film, close a wonderful sponsorship deal, fill every seat in the theatre and you will be hailed as a success. Follow this by missing a deadline, falling short of financial targets or creating a box office flop and it can be difficult to get your previous record to count for anything. To a certain extent, these workers are the most vulnerable in the production process. They cannot discount failures as simply moments when their artistic work has gone unappreciated by the audience, as the creatives might do, nor can they explain a downturn in popularity as a blip in an otherwise positive programme of events as executives and senior managers might do. The difference between success and failure is clear to all throughout the arts and media sectors and you can be sure that any failure will be fully analysed by the rest of the industry.

Getting a top job in one of these areas requires a dedicated and meticulous approach to work. You can't afford to cut corners or shirk your responsibility. You have to acknowledge the pressure and indeed, you have to love that pressure. You need to be able to work to deadlines, to work with other people and to be sure that when you delegate responsibility to workers below you, the work will be done to a quality you would expect and of which you will be proud. The work will take up a considerable amount of your time, and even when you're not 'on the job' you may find yourself obsessing about it or trying to work out problems that you can't do anything about at that moment in time. While these may appear to be reasons why not to take this kind of work, they are equally reasons why you do the job. You want to contribute to the world of the arts and media, to tell the stories you have found to the viewers, listeners and readers and to make sure they are positively received.

5 The management

If you are aiming for a top job in the management of an arts organ-isation you must be sure this is absolutely what you want to do. If you have ambitions to be a creative artist, a producer, or director, then don't work towards a management position. Management does not suit everyone; it requires skills that do not necessarily match the skill set of the artistically inclined person. Sometimes it can seem promotion and progression in the arts and media industry only exists in stepping up the management hierarchy, but it should always be remembered that every step up the management ladder also means a step away from hands-on creative work. Take a management job for the wrong reasons and you could set yourself up for frustration or failure as you find your skills are wasted or are at least unsuited to management tasks.

Similarly, if you are primarily motivated by tackling management issues and don't mind what sector you work in, you would also do well to steer clear of the arts. In other industry sectors management roles attract greater remuneration, greater rewards, sometimes greater prestige and profile, and they are usually roles that are a lot easier and a lot less pressurised than those within the arts sector.

The reason for this is simple. Since arts activities tend to be treated as a luxury rather than a necessity, arts organisations are usually operating in an under-funded environment. Consequently, arts venues, orchestras, theatres and galleries must carry out their work with limited resources. In the wider world of business, if there is a problem to be solved or a new initiative introduced to an organisation, there are usually substantial financial resources ready to be channelled behind that issue or initiative. In the arts, it is more a question of finding a solution that has the effect you desire, but that does not entail any great expense.

86

Senior managers are the people at the top of arts and media organisations who direct the ongoing work and future direction of these organisations. They may work for companies producing TV and radio programmes that must be attractive to the commissioning editors at the broadcast companies. They may work for organisations producing print-based information services or Internet services that are relied upon by individuals, businesses or special interest groups. They may be in charge of public-funded arts venues or theatre companies, where it must be clear that the programme set out season by season represents good value for the public's money. They may be in charge of programming or commissioning programmes for broadcast or for performance within an arts venue.

As a senior manager you are responsible for the resources that come into your organisation – financial, personnel and other – and to ensure they are used and managed efficiently. Providing solutions can be a challenge since it usually means getting more productivity out of the limited resources you have. You may need your staff to take on more responsibility or work longer hours without being able to offer increased remuneration or even job security. Your staff will no doubt already be working long hours under perhaps basic working conditions and yet you will need to motivate them to achieve the organisation's targets.

Mark Thompson, Director of Television, BBC

Mark Thompson freely admits that his career path has been unusual and is certainly one that few people would be able to follow today. However, his experience and views on the current state of the TV industry suggest that this should not prevent future employees from attaining high-flying jobs. Indeed, he believes that in the future there will be far less emphasis on background, education and career continuity for gaining a high-profile job and more chance for individuals with strong programme ideas to win through and enjoy top jobs.

Thompson joined the BBC's graduate training scheme straight out of university – an achievement that in itself was something akin to winning the lottery, since it took only around a dozen trainees and was oversubscribed by many high-flying candidates. The scheme centred on news and current affairs and while it included some formal training activities, the principal learning experience occurred on the job through a series of attachments to a wide range of programmes. Looking at the top level of managers in the BBC today – the programme commissioners, the station controllers and so on – many have current affairs, news and journalistic backgrounds, even Greg Dyke, the BBC's director general. Thompson wonders whether this isn't something to do with the propensity for these staff to be proactive – to go out of their way to find new and exciting stories and to work determinedly to make their programmes happen. At the same time it should be noted that it could simply be because there are more journalistic training courses centred around the broadcast media, so it provides an easier way in than trying to specialise in drama or a different programme genre.

Moving into management

Working his way through many programmes as a researcher, assistant producer and producer, Thompson had spent over a decade working on current affairs programmes when he decided to move his career forward and into management. He was appointed head of features at the BBC. Having already taken senior editing roles as an output editor for both *Newsnight* and *Panorama*, he was used to a high level of responsibility as well as managing the work of other journalists in order to produce high-quality programmes. Now he was in charge of 200 people and responsible for overseeing the creation of programmes such as *Crimewatch*, *Watchdog* and *Holiday*. He was even involved in the original commissioning of *Have I Got News For You*, which, while produced by an independent TV company, came under the responsibility of his department.

Moving around the BBC, Thompson has gained knowledge and experience of managing the organisation under a number of different remits. Having worked as head of factual programmes, he become controller of BBC2, taking overall responsibility for commissioning and scheduling the channel. He then moved again to be Director of Nations and Regions – a job that involved the management of some 4,000 staff distributed over 60 or 70 different sites nationwide. Finally, he was brought in as Director of Television by Greg Dyke when the latter became director general. In his current post, Thompson is responsible for output across the BBC's portfolio of TV channels.

Identifying good programmes

In spite of his rise through the organisation and away from programme making itself, Thompson is lucky, since his work today still feels as hands-on and as creative as it did when he was directly involved in producing shows. In a way, as Director of Television, he feels closer to the programmes now than he ever did as head of a department. In his role as Director of Nations and Regions, for example, he was dealing with large-scale management issues – budgets, personnel policy such as pay and remuneration – and trying to deal with those issues across a large workforce. Now, however, he feels his work is centred on identifying good programme ideas and enabling the programme makers to realise those ideas. While he has 16 or 17 people reporting to him – station controllers, schedulers and commissioners – it is up to him to provide feedback and guidance on deciding what is appropriate for each channel. He has a general overview across the BBC's entire output, but still finds himself viewing videos of programmes to assess whether they are the right thing for a particular channel at a particular time or discussing whether _The Weakest Link_ should be given a prime time BBC1 slot.

Naturally he still needs to address certain issues to do with the day-to-day running of the corporation, but on the whole his job is simply focused on making good TV. This is not to say it is an easy job – on the contrary, Thompson is adamant that a senior management position in any TV company is tough. 'The task of managers in these organisations is very difficult', he explains. 'At the end of the day we don't have anything to manage other than talent. The whole exercise is about somehow trying to nurture, encourage, shape or help shape creative talent.'

Doing this within an institution such as the BBC is not plain sailing, especially given the increasingly fragmentary nature of the sector. According to Thompson, using the traditional hierarchical structure for managing programme makers is simply not practical and will not produce programmes loved by today's audiences. Programmes can never be created by a production line approach – even separate episodes within complete series may be made by different people using different resources in entirely different ways. Add into this the challenges presented by new media and technology – the ever-expanding number of media channels plus the ease with which anyone with a bright idea can get a camera, point it in the right direction and make their own film – and it is obvious that any organisation that wishes to use the talent available and deliver good programmes can only do so by maximising its own flexibility.

The facilitator

Rather than trying to impose some sort of order or 'Right Way of Doing Things' across the company, Thompson believes it is management's responsibility to ensure the programme makers are able to make their programmes in the best way possible. This can mean challenging ideas about programme making itself: 'One job of senior management is to be an irritant or a catalyst', he says. 'It is as much about going round shaking things up and disrupting things as it is about saying "you haven't followed the guidelines". It's not obvious that management should increase stability – sometimes it's the reverse of that.'

At this point in time Thompson believes the most subversive person at the BBC is Greg Dyke – the man at the top. He cites the move to take the Nine o'Clock News to the Ten o'Clock slot as an example of the BBC injecting instability and challenge throughout the TV industry rather than simply restricting the challenge to within their own organisation. In this kind of atmosphere, Thompson believes the 'awkward customer' will be the one who succeeds, rather than the conventional character. In other words, if you want to take a maverick approach to programme making, to directing or producing, now is probably the best time to make your move since the industry is extremely open to new ideas and ways of making TV.

Thompson notes that all senior managers need to have excellent communication skills and be at least a little charismatic if they are to inspire and encourage people. However, he notes that ultimately managers must enjoy managing. They must get a kick out of working with policies, budgets, and so on. This is not a role to be taken lightly and certainly there have been examples of good programme-makers being incredibly unhappy and ineffective within management roles. At the same time, he notes that it is practically impossible for someone who is merely interested in the task of management to be successful in the media. Without loving the industry and the whole idea of programme making, there are too many concurrent frustrations or barriers to pure management work. It should also be clear that working for the BBC is a completely different task to working for a commercial broadcast station or independent production company. 'For independent companies, ultimately the agenda is about driving revenue and making profits and so they spend time addressing those matters', he notes. 'Our objective here is to make good programmes and give them to the public. That is all.'

Thompson began by noting how his career progression would be very difficult to match today. Not only would it entail being successful in applying for a traineeship, but it would also hinge on moving within the BBC in a way that is extremely difficult if not impossible today. Instead, it is more likely that senior managers will rise through the ranks across a number of different employers rather than just through one company.

Job (in)security continues

To be effective in a senior management role you must regard the arts as a necessity rather than a luxury. You must be able to argue for your cause, to ensure your organisation gets the recognition it deserves and more importantly the funding and financial support it requires. If you do not consider your organisation to be integral to the lives of the community it serves, you will not be able to provide the vision and drive the organisation requires.

It should also be clear that within some arts organisations, the fact that you have reached a position at senior management level does not necessarily mean you have finally attained complete job security. A high-profile job puts you in the eye of the press and media, so any suggestion or evidence of mismanagement within the organisation could lead to your downfall. In extreme cases you may be asked to leave the organisation simply to draw a line under a particularly difficult chapter in the organisation's history. A high-profile development project may misfire through no fault of your own but it will appear that public funds have been wasted. If you are operating at the top of your profession, you must accept the full implications of that responsibility.

In some organisations, senior managers may always find themselves fire-fighting – defending the organisation and trying to give it a secure and certain existence – rather than being proactive in moving the company forward. Indeed, some appointments to senior management may be made specifically because those people are thought to have the skills required to save an arts organisation. It may be that an organisation needs repositioning in terms of its work or public image in order to continue in the future. There may be serious problems with the internal functions of the organisation and the way in which work is carried out. While such work is challenging and exciting, it also exerts a high level of pressure on senior managers to have a clear and positive impact as soon as they start working for the organisation.

Looking ahead

Forward planning is crucial to good business but is also something that can only be carried out by companies who have financial security. If you are certain you will be in business five years from now, then you can put initiatives in place to determine what your organisation will be doing at that time. If you don't know whether you will be operating five years from now, then all your energy and time will be spent trying to guarantee you will be functioning.

While the above may be true for publicly funded arts organisations, there are still arts-oriented companies and certainly media-related companies that operate almost entirely along usual business lines. Record companies, publishing companies, and independent radio and TV companies may offer similar challenges as are found within manufacturing and service industries. They are dealing with a product that can be developed, packaged and sold to customers. Senior management will therefore be dedicated to finding ways of making this operation efficient while trying to produce a high-quality product. This can mean tracking down the best talent for a record label, or finding the right presenter to take on an important radio programme.

The main difference between these companies and those in other parts of industry is that few other companies have the same need for a good public profile. Few companies rely on public taste and opinion for success in the way a record company or a book publisher does. If their author or musician is flavour of the month, receives good press coverage and so on, the company will be successful. If the artists they promote are not popular and do not inspire customers to go and buy their work, it is not just the artist who will feel the effects but the company itself.

93

Charlie Harris, Co-director of a small music company

Charlie Harris' career has been absolutely tied to the rise in popularity of the club scene throughout the UK and internationally. Over the past decade and more the club culture has grown out of the outlawed warehouse rave parties of the early 90s to be a multi-million pound leisure industry. Harris, together with his business partners at Serious Records, has seen the small company grow from purely DJ management work to an events and promotion company and finally to a record label in its own right.

Harris notes that he has been very fortunate to have had friends working in the music business whom he could get involved with, but then since he's always been interested in clubbing it seems hardly surprising that he should find himself involved in the business. The company consists of three friends who have known each other since they went to school together. Harris and his friends were always the enterprising type, setting up money-making schemes whenever they could throughout their childhood.

Having taken a BTEC HND course in business and finance when he left school, Harris set up his own property management company in the south of London. His best friend from school was brother to Judge Jules – one of the leading DJs within the club scene of the early 1990s. As demand for Jules increased, Jules' brother became his manager – driving him to gigs and taking care of his bookings. He effectively took what was an informal and ad hoc activity and turned it into a business venture whereby Jules could be managed properly. The arrangement brought a more professional approach to the club scene – payments were guaranteed, Jules' reputation increased and with that increase in reputation, it was possible to increase his appearance fee.

The work with Jules enabled the operation to expand. With such a high profile DJ already on their books, the fledgling company attracted other DJs and signed management deals with them too, each time offering to manage their entire careers – from bookings to promotion and press enquiries.

The company had soon signed up important figures from across the club scene including Norman Jay, Graham Gold and Sonique. Just as Serious began to expand, Harris left the property business and took a management role at Serious, working alongside people he knew in an industry he loved.

Expanding the business

As the club scene expanded, so too did Serious' activities. The company used their own DJs for private parties, and as a result of this decided that they should expand their activities into event management and promotion. They started arranging club nights, which worked to promote their own DJs as well as creating an image for the company itself and producing more revenue. Serious now run monthly nights at locations around the UK.

The move into record publishing was a natural evolution. Sonique had already enjoyed some success in the pop industry, singing with an early dance act called S-Express. Now teamed up with Judge Jules, she frequently sang live over his mixes at nightclubs. Jules returned the favour by teaching Sonique how to mix music herself and, together with another of the company's directors, Sonique wrote and released a single that had massive success in the clubs and ended up taking the number one chart position for three weeks. By signing a deal with a large international music company, Serious are now able to record and promote their own artists in a competitive and professional manner. Having enjoyed chart success, the company are poised to promote their artists in a concerted way over the next few months and years.

Careful planning

Harris notes that while each of these expansions – into events and then into the record label – have constituted risks to the company, each step has been taken according to good business sense and careful planning. 'Every aspect of running the company has been a challenge', he says. 'Whenever we've tried something new we've always been careful to see that it works and progressed that way. The important thing is not to do anything which has major adverse effects on the company if it doesn't work out. If it does work then great, but you have to know what's going to happen next if it doesn't.'

To this extent, running the company has a great deal to do with common business sense rather than specific knowledge of how the music industry works. 'You can have loads of great ideas about what you want to do,' notes Harris, 'but unless you know how to put them into practice and you know the pitfalls, you can get into trouble. You have to know when to get legal advice regarding contracts, for example, or when to get an outside graphics agency to produce your material. The tendency is to try and save money and do everything in-house, but that isn't always the right thing to do.'

Indeed, bringing professionalism to the clubbing scene appears to have been the secret of Serious' success. The scene may have lost some of its rebellious image, but it has become one of the most popular leisure pursuits for 18- to 25-year-olds. One-and-a-half million people go clubbing every weekend and these are people who will spend their disposable income on clothes, records and other merchandise that ties in with that activity. Serious may be a respected and commercial business but it is operating in an area where customer tastes and industry trends can move extremely quickly. The success of the business so far has been its ability to be flexible, to key into the demands of the paying public and continue to exist at the heart of the club scene. This hasn't so much been a strategic goal, but a position that has happened naturally as the people behind the company have been leading lights in the industry itself.

Keeping high profile

Harris' day-to-day job is essentially to manage Judge Jules. This extends beyond managing the DJ's diary – which is usually completely full eight to nine months in advance – to sorting out all travel arrangements for Jules, accommodation and so on, as well as ensuring the places where he appears are suitable for him. Maintaining Jules' high profile means ensuring he only plays a certain level of event. If Harris is approached by a club promoter to book Jules for a new club night, he will send a different DJ there first, just to ensure the club is well run. Harris also liaises with the broadcasters who employ Jules to do radio shows and special mixes, and with the press – including the specialist print media that has sprung up around the club scene. Maintaining all these contacts enables Harris to keep abreast of the club scene, to see what's coming up and what's happening, information that he can feed back into the company and into managing Judge Jules' own activities.

Alongside this, Harris has responsibilities to the company and developing its business. Planning ahead is a little difficult for the operation. On the one hand, predicting trends in the club scene isn't easy, while on the other hand the company is only now financially in a position where the directors can start thinking strategically about where they want to be in five years' time rather than concentrating on the effective day-to-day running of the operation. Harris has also been responsible for employing new members of the team at Serious. It's a small company – around 10 or so employees – and finding the right people has been crucial to making the company work.

As Harris points out, while it may be attractive to bring in people who know the club scene and have a high level of knowledge about what's happening, it is unwise to bring in someone who just wants to go out clubbing every single night. 'Clubbing can be destructive, and it's no good employing someone who won't make it in to work on Monday morning or who always wants to leave early on Fridays', he says. Serious' employees work very hard and usually long hours, so they need to be motivated by the area of work itself. The prospect of free flights and free entry into clubs at Ibiza every year is certainly a bonus few other companies can offer.

'There are two main qualities you need to work at this level and they're both related to interpersonal skills', says Harris.

'One is that you need to be noticed by people. You have to have an impact on those around you – whether that means the people you are working with or the industry in general. The second aspect is that you need a certain number of contacts within the industry. If you're trying to set up your own company you certainly need those contacts because it's very difficult to be taken seriously otherwise.'

Harris certainly believes that success lies in attitude and determination. But while the company has now reached the size where they can bring in new people in reception roles and develop them through the company, other roles do require qualifications. The company employs a dedicated accountant, for example, who took a pay cut to take the job following his previous corporate employer. He was more than happy to do this, however, as he wanted to work in the club industry. Harris recommends that whether seeking a high-flying job within the music industry or setting up your own company or record label, you should always spend some time in a straightforward job within the industry to ensure it is something you want to be involved in. The work requires 100 per cent dedication and what appears glossy and attractive from the outside can prove to be less fun on the inside.

Perpetual innovation

Few companies are as flexible or as consistently innovative in their work as organisations in the arts and media world. Management must constantly challenge the way work is carried out to ensure the organisation makes the best use of resources and takes advantage of the opportunities open to it. A record company may need to completely reinvent an artist in order to sell their recordings. They may need to create an entirely new department to address a new genre of music as it develops. A buildings-based theatre company may need to rearrange its work processes and employees in order to facilitate a national tour. A TV company may need to change the way its production staff work together in order to create a new series or type of programme.

In each case, strong management is required to ensure that resources within the organisation are realised and channelled effectively towards the priorities for that organisation. If realising this goal means significant changes to the work of others, senior management must provide support for those employees to make the changes required. The arts and media industries can take nothing for granted – at least in the manufacturing sector or even in a bank, a company can rely on a certain level of demand for their products without having to repackage or relaunch them every couple of months.

Huge challenges

A senior management role within a private company or well-established institution can bring a degree of stability to a career. After all, you will be employed on a long-term contract and it is less likely that the organisation you work for will be subject to substantial fluctuations in its financial position or customer interest. However, this does not mean your job will be static. At the moment, parts of the arts world are facing huge challenges that could change absolutely the way they operate, create art and communicate with their audience.

In the music industry, for example, much discussion has centred around the use of the Internet for sharing music files. Technology has made it possible for music to be shared without the artist or record company receiving any revenue. According to one source, the industry probably has around 10 years to come to terms with this technology; that is the time it will take before the general music-buying public decide it is easy, acceptable and just as good to download an album from the Internet as it is to walk to the local record shop and buy it on CD or vinyl.

There are similar problems in other art forms. The film industry has embraced the Internet as a platform for showcasing short films by new talent, but could it become the ultimate platform for full-length releases in the future? Will Internet channels become serious competitors to terrestrial, digital, satellite and cable TV? If so, what are the implications for today's broadcasting companies, especially if independent production companies decide they can set up their own channels relatively easily.

The print media has also undergone huge changes with the introduction of technology in the production process. Desktop publishing has reduced costs and changed the face of the industry entirely. What will be the future of print as the Internet becomes more accessible and easy to use?

All these issues must be considered by the senior management of any arts organisation. And rather than encouraging their organisation to plough on regardless, they must encourage them to be innovative, to take on and respond to evolving technologies and to use them proactively. One of the biggest challenges is to provide a safe creative space where the artists and producers can work and succeed. Insisting that creatives stick to the guidelines or produce only one kind of performance will be fatal to the future of any organisation. While having an awareness of where the organisation has come from, what it is good at and the wider context of the history of work within that particular artistic sector, senior management have to be innovative and responsive to change. Allowing responsiveness and flexibility throughout an artistic organisation is a creative challenge far in excess of anything you'll find in the manufacturing industry.

Keeping in touch

Even an institution such as the BBC faces serious challenges that could change its work in the future. The company must create a strategy that will preserve its status within the industry in spite of the proliferation of new digital and Internet broadcasting services. So while you may assume your status within an arts organisation affords you some security, you certainly cannot relax within your role. If you aren't asking major questions about the work and direction of your organisation, you are not doing your job properly.

For this reason, senior managers need to be in touch with market trends and audience demands in a meticulous and detailed way. If the senior managers are to lead their organisations in a successful and lucrative direction, they need to know what trends are emerging both within their audience and within their part of the industry. Are there new programme ideas that should be developed? What's the latest technology to aid publishing or

Web development? Since it is impossible for one person to know all these things, senior managers must be excellent networkers and communicators. They must be able to take ideas and information from all parts of the sector in which they work – from industry commentators, from their own staff and even from their own financial supporters – and use this information for the good of their organisations.

Lorna Clarke – Senior management in national radio

Lorna Clarke has worked in radio for over 16 years. Describing her background as 'quite formal', she took a radio course at a London polytechnic after school, a practical course that included placements and work experience within the BBC and independent local radio. The course was a news-based one, and while Clarke had little interest in becoming a journalist she took the course because it was the only way to get into radio and acquire the skills and knowledge she needed. Clarke's real interest lay in the creation of music programmes, but there was no training ground for this side of the media's output.

Placements took Clarke around the country from Cornwall to Humberside to Newcastle, and finally back to a job at Radio London. The last job was exciting, not just because it meant Clarke was working on her home turf, but also because, at the time, there were limited options for people who wanted to work on music-led radio stations. Radio London was developing the market for popular music, playing American hip hop and featuring many guest musicians and DJs from the United States. Clarke's first position at the station was working in the newsroom and developing a magazine show, and even here she was gaining important practical skills that would put her in good stead for the future.

Radio London then went through a metamorphosis and finally re-emerged as Greater London Radio or GLR (since renamed London Live). Clarke remained at the station and was also able to get involved in projects further afield through the BBC's World Service programmes. At one point she worked on a live news show broadcast to the Caribbean at a time when the area was in the throws of political turmoil.

Kiss FM

Around this time, a pirate radio station, Kiss FM, successfully bid for an official broadcasting licence and consequently became a legitimate radio station. They contacted Clarke and, impressed by her experience plus her knowledge of London's music and club scene, invited her to join the company. The task Clarke and her fellow workers were charged with was essentially to build the new radio station from scratch. There was no company history to the station, no hierarchy of management or programmers to determine how things should be done, by whom or when. Within the first six months of her working for the station, Kiss FM signed a deal with a major drinks company and as a result Clarke was asked to organise live outside broadcasts in five different US cities to occur in three months' time as a competition tie-in. This was all very well, but at that point the company hadn't even hired a full-time engineer.

Clarke notes that had she spent any time considering the enormity of this project there's little chance that she would have attempted the tie-in broadcasts, let alone run them successfully. However, she rose to the challenge and learnt quickly. It was an opportunity that clearly would never have arisen for her within the corridors of the BBC.

Kiss FM was one of the first radio stations to conscientiously tap into the contemporary dance music scene and reflect the emerging club culture. Clarke notes that this was not a particularly strategic or business-driven move on the part of Kiss, but it happened simply because the music was there and that was what interested their listeners. The DJs who played in the clubs were more than willing to do their sets on the radio and as a result Kiss were able to build the station's reputation through the popularity of the dance music itself. Clarke received an award for programming for her work at Kiss and found herself promoted to the board of directors – a move she certainly wasn't expecting, although it seems clear she had played – and was continuing to play – a crucial role in the development of the station.

Kiss then sent Clarke out to South Africa, where it was suggested the station could extend its brand. Clarke had always wanted to travel to Africa, and was very to keen to work here. At the time the country had one of the best demographics for a young black male audience – an audience who were certainly interested in hip hop and dance music. Having carried out sufficient research, it was decided the project would not work in the way the company had first envisaged.

Headhunted

The BBC headhunted Clarke into her current position as head of mainstream programming for Radio 1. In this position, she is responsible for the producers and presenters across the roster of mainstream radio shows produced by Radio 1 – from the breakfast show through to the late night show. She works alongside two other programmers – one for live music and one for specialist programming – and reports directly to the overall station controller. While this work has meant she has now moved away from the hands-on creative side of production – putting a programme together, sorting out the playlist and creating the on-air sound of a show – the work is still creative.

'There has to be a lot of creative input here or it wouldn't be as attractive a job for me', she says. 'But it's creative in a different way.' She is enthusiastic, for example, about the way in which she has gone about recruiting people to work for the station – the selection of six new trainees, for example, side-stepped the more traditional recruitment process in order to identify people who would not usually come into contact with the BBC, much less find themselves able to contribute to its radio output. It is also part of her remit to ensure that the people employed within her team receive the best opportunities for fulfilling their own creative potential, thereby benefiting the station and the corporation as a whole.

As well as being a high-level manager, Clarke is a team player, consulting with producers, DJs and others on campaigns and themes that may be pushed by the station at a particular time. There may be a 'Summer of Guitars' one year or a series of information programmes centring on students or more general issues such as poverty or sexuality. She is also responsible for appointing new DJs to specific time slots. Having launched two breakfast shows, she knows how critical it is to pitch the show and presenter correctly in order to appeal to the right audience.

New music

Another area she particularly enjoys is being involved in the discovery of new genres of music and the way in which each genre interacts. She must decide, for example, whether the station recognises R'n'B as mainstream music rather than a specialist genre, and how this should influence the overall sound of the station. Getting this right is a matter of being aware of current trends and matching these demands as well as being a leading voice in forming opinions. It's a difficult balance to make – misjudge the impact of a presenter or one part of the music policy and the whole station risks losing credibility with the listeners.

When Clarke first came to the BBC the company was undergoing a radical change in terms of how it was managed and run. It wasn't too long ago that Radio 1 itself underwent an intensive and stressful relaunch which followed the termination of many well-established DJ's shows. To some extent, however, Clarke feels her lack of knowledge about how the station worked previously and lack of experience of working within the corporation's hierarchy as it then existed has benefited her career. 'It actually helps if you don't know how the BBC works,' she says, 'because that means you have a more fearless approach to the organisation. You're not afraid of knocking on doors or telling people what you want to do. Once you're in you can then prove your worth through the work you do.'

Clarke believes that the proliferation of channels through digital broadcasting and Internet radio can only offer more opportunities for aspiring arts and media workers to get stuck in and show their ability to prospective employers and the industry in general. Just as her career at Kiss FM received a boost with the growth in popularity of hip hop, dance and club music, many people who want to make a big noise in this part of the media are wise to align themselves with a particular genre of music and to promote themselves as the specialist exponents of that sound.

Getting to the top

Without exception, those who reach the highest level of management in arts and media organisations do so through exceptional and extensive careers that span their chosen art form and sometimes span a range of different art forms. They have taken work across disciplines within their sector, acquiring on-the-job experience, a full understanding of how the industry works and a sufficiently high level of confidence that they can work effectively in this environment. They will have gleaned all they can from formal training courses whether they be internal training and development initiatives or externally held events. They may have planned their ascent strategically – identifying areas of work they need to experience, new skills they require and so on. They may have been identified as high-flyers by their own organisation's personnel function and developed in order to meet the skill requirements of the future. They may have simply followed the opportunities that their career has offered, ulti-mately finding that they have developed the skills required for work at a senior level.

While ensuring that every part of their company and organi-sation has the best resources and skills available for its effective operation, this level of management may also be responsible for providing an identifiable figurehead for that organisation within the arts and media industry. Senior managers may be called upon to give keynote speeches at press conferences or public meetings. They may be referred to for comment on industry trends. They will certainly be called to respond if their organisation steps into areas of controversy, whether it be an organisation spending public funds or a private company deemed to have exceeded the realms of good taste in their latest activities.

While the administrative and production roles described in the previous chapter still have a degree of hands-on influence on the final output from their company – whether it be a TV production company, a publisher or a theatre company, this level of management are at another remove from the chalk face. They need to take a strategic view of the organisation's work, consider where the most lucrative or popular areas of operation might be, what audience trends should be addressed or prepared for and how to fulfil the organisation's artistic agenda in the future. This requires a complete and detailed understanding of the sector in which the organisation operates, the audience it is serving and the way the organisation works.

The complexity of these jobs depends fully on the employing organisation. The managing director of an orchestra will deal with different issues to those of the programming manager of a radio station or a senior manager in the BBC. Whether the organisation is a private concern or publicly funded will also have a large part to play in the overall management style required. Private companies are operated in order to maximise profits and maintain shareholder confidence. If you are working for a publicly funded organisation it is necessary to have a strong understanding of the political implications of your work and how to ensure you can get the best value from those limited public funds.

Breda Daly – Director of development in the theatre

Breda Daly was always interested in the theatre. Growing up in Dublin, the theatre was part of the culture around her, but while she appreciated and admired the amount of personal involvement many actors and artists put into their performances and productions, she was not disposed to working in this way herself. She did not feel she was creative and could not see herself working as an actress or designer, for example. While she knew other people who found work in the industry through their devotion to the arts, she took a job in a bank in Dublin, prioritising instead the need for a steady and secure career, which at that time even offered the prospect of a pension. Five years later, she realised the banking industry was not for her. Still with a passion for the theatre, but without the conviction that she could work in this area, she took a degree in English and psychology, a course that she chose purely to satisfy her artistic interests.

Having completed the course, Breda travelled for a year and then moved to London. Her travelling experience had improved her self-confidence and gave her more courage when considering her career options. Having seen a couple of productions at the then new Almeida Theatre in Islington, she wrote to the theatre expressing an interest to work for them in some capacity. At interview it was decided that her financial and business background made her the ideal person to start a fund-raising initiative for the theatre. This function was a completely new start for the Almeida and so Breda, along with the rest of the team, effectively made up a strategy and approach to fund-raising from scratch.

With a number of Americans on the board of the theatre, the first and most obvious approach was one used in the US whereby current audience members are approached to give more money in order to become 'Friends' of the theatre. For an annual donation, individuals are given incentives such as preferential booking arrangements, regular programme updates and newsletters and even the occasional special function. Once this initiative was up and running, the company looked closely at developing the corporate side of the equation, trying to find big businesses who would offer substantial funding to the theatre in exchange for brand and name placement within the venue and its publications. A third method of funding was to research and apply to the wide range of grant-making trusts that were in a position to help the theatre.

People skills

Throughout this time Daly was given only one formal training course on corporate persuasion and communications, run through the Association of Business and the Arts scheme – now known as Arts and Business. While this aided her negotiation skills and offered techniques to approaching possible funders or writing letters of application, the majority of her work was simply a matter of learning effective techniques as she went along. 'Fund-raising is a people skill', she maintains. 'You need to know how to get on well with people and find ways of appealing to them in order to secure their financial support.'

To this extent, Daly argues, the work is extremely creative. Devising new ways of raising money for specific programmes or for the core funding of an arts organisation is always a challenge. While it may be possible to make similar approaches to similar potential sponsors, every case will be unique as the sponsorship package has to be tailored for the preferences and requirements of each organisation approached. In many ways, Daly must understand the priorities of the organisation she is approaching as well as she understands her own organisation's priorities in order to key into their requirements and produce a mutually satisfying deal.

Daly spent nine years at the Almeida, during which she was very successful in bringing in funds to support the theatre's work. She then felt it was time to move on and find a more rounded position with new challenges, which is when the opportunity for head of fund-raising at the National Theatre appeared. Here, Daly has a team of 12 fund-raisers and as part of the senior management team she finds herself using more basic management skills in facilitating that team to reach the funding targets required rather than through her own hands-on fund-raising skills.

'The job is still satisfying – more so really, because everything is so much bigger', she says. 'We have a bigger team working on fund-raising and as an organisation we are able to pull in more money. The job is all about planning and using our opportunities to assess what we can do to increase finance levels.' As at the Almeida, funding is sought for core practices – the general running of the theatre itself – as well as for individual productions. Daly and her team can use specific shows or events within the theatre to lever funds from a wide range of organisations towards their core activities.

At the same time, Daly is working to move fund-raising activities and the awareness of this part of the process closer to the centre of the organisation. In other words, when a new season is drawn up or certain actors are brought into the theatre, they are made aware of the need for fund-raising so that strategies can be created at the earliest possible stage to exploit the opportunities each event offers. 'The main role of the fund-raiser is to be the facilitator between someone who wants to give money to an arts organisation and the organisation that needs it', explains Daly. 'The donators don't want to talk to me, and aren't that interested in meeting me, but they are interested in meeting actors and directors.'

This leads to the second and equally important half of Daly's work – managing the people who work within the National Theatre itself. Donators are willing to give money and support in return for initiatives such as special events or meeting the high-profile artists at the theatre. Actors and directors may therefore agree to meet sponsors either formally or informally – perhaps meeting their representatives after a show. Obviously, these activities must not interfere with the artist's primary function, which is to create a high-quality performance, so Daly and her team are expert at coordinating the desires of the sponsors with the availability of the theatre's personnel in order to secure mutually beneficial funding arrangements.

A suitable sponsor

In securing the cooperation of the theatre's artists, Daly needs to ensure that potential funders are suitable for and acceptable to the theatre. A lucrative deal might be attractive but it could come from a source regarded with suspicion by the artists or the wider arts world. Big business is very interested in being allied with the arts because such an arrangement can cast businesses in a positive light and even help to deflect negative criticism of business practices. If the artists themselves are not happy with being supported by sponsoring organisations, Daly could create a situation as negative as if the funding were not there in the first place. To help ensure that this doesn't happen, Daly has brought high-profile artists from the theatre on to the board of the fund-raising department, where they can provide input at an early stage and help to steer the department's activities.

Daly works to both long- and short-term targets. At any one time she is guiding her department towards securing finance for activities some three years down the road – a strategy that requires substantial up-front planning. Her job is also regarded as a fairly tough one in the industry, not only is the line between success and failure clear – either you reach your funding targets or you don't – but also any shortfall will have direct and clear repercussions on the ability of the theatre to produce quality performances. 'You're only as good as your last deal', says Daly. 'It is a highly pressurised job, but then there are pressures in any job. With fund-raising you can prepare yourself for approaching a client and be prepared until you're blue in the face, but there's still a chance that that funding will not happen. You have some control over the outcome, but it has to be said it's not a lot of control.'

In spite of the comparatively hard-nosed business approach to work in this area, Daly is adamant that fund-raising is first and foremost a people skill. If you have a good product to sell, it can be very enjoyable getting to know the structure and priorities of a potential sponsor, and then finding ways of securing their involvement in the production of art within your own organisation.

Getting to know the culture

Senior managers need a firm understanding of the organisational culture in which they are working. Large organisations will, by their very nature, rely on hierarchical structures and standard processes to get work done. The way in which the BBC operates, for example, in developing programme ideas from the creative's first inspiration through to funding its development, the production of a pilot episode and finally broadcasting the full series will be different to the process followed by a small production company. No doubt there will be similar stages in the exercise along the way and at the end of the day the result will be similar, but getting to that point will involve different parts of the organisation and a myriad of different people. At senior management level, it is possible to influence exactly how this work is done. You may decide there is a better way to run the production process, one that increases the flexibility available to creatives carrying out their work. This may simply require an adjustment of current practices or it may mean a complete overhaul of the process. In both cases you will need to know how the organisation currently operates in order to introduce this new way of working.

That said, it is not uncommon to find a senior manager appointed to an arts organisation within a sector he or she has not worked in before. On occasions like these the organisation has appointed this person specifically because of their management talents rather than their experience in the sector. The new managing director of an opera company, for example, may have no previous record of working in opera, but they will have had experience of working in a similar-sized organisation and dealt with the same issues of operating a creative company effectively. The managing director will not be completely ignorant of the art genre – they will at least have a good knowledge of the art form, albeit based on personal interest rather than work experience.

Charisma

Given the job requirements of providing a good public profile and being able to influence the work of others throughout the organisation, senior managers must be reasonably charismatic. It is not enough to be technically good at the job, one must be able to project a likeable and inspiring personality – one that will unite the organisation and leave a lasting impression on the media. While the senior manager of a manufacturing or service business may be selected for his or her steady and conventional approach to the industry, a dynamic and even maverick attitude can be a positive advantage within the arts and media industry. Certainly, senior arts and media managers should have the confidence and experience to implement initiatives and manage their organisation sensibly, but they must also be able to inspire and excite those around them.

Management at this level can still be creative but in a different way to that of the administrative, production or creative employees. Senior managers may not actually be responsible for a broadcast programme's look, feel and content, but they do influence the creation of that work. They might commission a certain programme, bring together individuals to work on a piece or give input on how the work should be promoted and sold. They are responsible for the image of the organisation and even for managing the expectations of its audiences. The senior management of a theatre company, for example, can decide whether the company will be perceived as moving in a new and innovative direction, or whether they are a traditional, safe-bet production company.

Being creative at this level means realising objectives through the work of others. You might enable a production team to realise their creative vision or bring together a group of performers and directors who will meet the theatre company's stated aim. Making these events happen brings you satisfaction rather than contributing directly to the event yourself.

Gary McKeone – Director of Literature, Arts Council of England

If Gary McKeone were writing a book on getting a top job in the arts and media, one chapter at least would have to be entitled 'Luck'. At first sight his career progression to Literature Officer at the Arts Council of England appears to have been a fairly straightforward one. He's had a number of different administration-related jobs in different organisations, picking up a great deal of new skills along the way and usually embarking on a very steep learning curve with each new appointment. However, his first step into a steady job in a high-profile arts organisation certainly had more to do with fortune and chance than it did with his being suitably qualified for the job.

With a degree in English and Spanish, McKeone was living in Derry, Ireland, where it was difficult to find any substantial work in the arts sector. With a passion for all forms of art, he ended up taking a wide variety of roles for different companies. He worked for local radio, reviewed plays for the broadcast and print media, helped to organise a literature festival and helped a theatre company, promoting their tour and even transporting cast and crew between venues. 'There were lots of small jobs to do, but it didn't really amount to anything', he says. At the end of the '80s, McKeone saw a _Guardian_ advertisement for a literature assistant to help organise a festival at the Royal Festival Hall (RFH). Feeling this was a good opportunity, he applied for the post.

The RFH informed all applicants that if they were called for interview, they would be informed by the end of the year. Meanwhile, McKeone and his partner decided they would make the move to London regardless of their employment status or the outcome of this application. The plan was to apply for work within the publishing industry once they had made the move to the city.

And so McKeone found himself walking the streets of London in the New Year, walking from publisher to publisher with his CV, being treated amicably enough, but not being offered any work. Having received no word from the RFH, he assumed that his application had been unsuccessful; however, his partner persuaded him to call into the South Bank Centre and introduce himself nevertheless, just in case there were other vacancies coming up. When he met the personnel staff at the RFH he discovered that the original job application process had been held up over the Christmas period. No letters had been sent out at all, and in fact he was among the shortlisted candidates who were to be invited in for interview.

Literature assistant at the Royal Festival Hall

McKeone was subsequently appointed literature assistant and for the next three years revelled in the work of creating the RFH as a prime venue for literature-related activities. He worked to build a programme of events, inviting writers to appear and read, linking these events with the centre's own bookshop and poetry library, and ensuring there would be an audience for every event. 'It became a primary venue in the literature world', he says. 'We were able to put on poetry festivals, promote new voices and feature writers who were just about to be published.'

The work provided a terrific grounding for McKeone. Not only was he working within an area for which he had a passion, but he gained a wealth of experience in all areas of arts administration. He was responsible for booking the writers, organising their transport and accommodation, proofreading the posters, managing the events on the day and ensuring the whole exercise came in on budget. To do all this he had to work with a wide range of arts organisations – from fund-awarding bodies to publishers.

Travelling theatre

Following this he was invited back to Ireland to become the company director for a travelling theatre company that featured some of Ireland's most renowned actors, writers and directors. McKeone notes that in spite of being invited to do this job, he had at that stage no experience in the day-to-day management of a theatre company at all. 'It was a very steep learning curve', he admits. 'When I started I had no experience in managing large budgets or securing sponsorship. I hadn't dealt with the Irish Arts Council before, but here I was making an application to them on the company's behalf.'

While working at this level, McKeone also had to oversee the day-to-day running of the company. In addition to ensuring the company was funded and could operate, he was responsible for posters and advertising at venues and even driving the crew and cast between performances. He enjoyed the work immensely, not least because of the great time to be had in the company of the actors and writers.

The Arts Council

The theatre company was, however, on its last legs and its final demise corresponded with the appearance of a temporary post within the literature department of the Arts Council of England. McKeone applied successfully and when his boss moved on his employment was extended. It was then a matter of continuing to work for the Council, gaining more experience and skills in order to be ready to take the directorship of the section when the post fell vacant. 'My one regret is that I didn't buy a lottery ticket during this time, because everything fell into place so well it was amazing', says McKeone. 'It was so much a case of being in the right place at the right time.'

One of McKeone's first jobs when he arrived at the Council was to act as touring officer for the literature department. The Council brought writers to the UK from overseas to promote their work. There were around five such programmes every year, each lasting about two weeks. This meant McKeone was spending a reasonable amount of time on the road with writers during the year – a job that he still can't quite believe he was lucky enough to land.

McKeone is certainly lucky to be able to work in the field of literature in this way. There are very few similar jobs in the literature world – unlike other art sectors such as music or the theatre, there are no significant national institutions dedicated to the promotion of literature other than the Arts Council itself. Publishing is a healthy, commercial business, but this area is more to do with securing profits than it is with promoting literature in general as an educational and social tool.

'It's really all been on-the-job learning', says McKeone. 'Within an institution like the Arts Council there are a number of training courses offered in terms of management and budgeting and so on, but the actual nitty-gritty of the job you pick up as you go along.' Certainly he has felt the emphasis on his work shift from hands-on to a more strategic role. Since becoming responsible for shaping the work of the literature department, not only is he concerned with the promotion of literature in the present day, he must also consider where literature will be in three and five years' time. He must think about the legacy that will be left to later generations and how people will view the literature of this century in the future. By expanding the accepted definition of literature outside the narrow image of simply poetry or highbrow novels, he believes he's dealing with the largest art form in the UK.

Readers and writers

The job is not simply about supporting writers, but about developing readers as well. McKeone notes that writing courses delivered by organisations such as the Arvon Foundation may occasionally produce a top-selling author, but the true value of running those courses lies in the development of the students as readers. 'We need to get across the message that reading itself is a creative act,' says McKeone, 'the reader completes the circle and is therefore of equal importance to the writer.'

'Certainly there are skills you need to work in this area', says McKeone. 'The administrative skills are important and institutions like this need good management skills but a lot of that is really common sense.' Business skills such as budgeting and financial management are in demand within the arts sector in general, but with the need for increased accountability for the spending of public funds, these skills are particularly useful in organisations such as the Arts Council. 'There has been a tendency in the past for organisations to be quite flabby in their approach to finance, but they really need to be run as businesses', says McKeone. 'There's always this idea that arts organisations say they're unique and can't be run in the same way as other companies, but in many respects they are. A play or a poetry evening is still a product. You can still market and manage that event in the same way you do with other products.'

But while business skills may be increasing in the sector, it is clear that a passion for the arts is crucial to a successful career in the sector. McKeone notes that his passion for literature sees him through when he's working long hours or has to deal with frustrating problems. 'If the people working in the sector weren't passionate about it, then the job becomes something that anyone can do', he notes. 'There wouldn't be the same spark about it and the returns from doing the job wouldn't be as great as they are.'

Managing discontinuity

One skill involved in the management of arts and media organisations recognised throughout industry and commerce is the ability to manage discontinuity. Even on a daily basis, the resources, finances and people senior managers deal with change and rearrange. A TV series will use different content between episodes, and may use the skills of different directors, performers and production staff. New theatre productions will use different actors, directors and designers. The production of a film will involve bringing together a unique combination of talented people to work together only on that one project. In each case it is senior management's responsibility to see that these individuals and resources work together effectively and productively.

Managing discontinuity is a matter of having a flexible approach to be able to meet the unique challenges of each new project, while being able to deliver a confident and all-encompassing vision that will unify the diverse elements of the production. It requires a great deal of energy so that every production gets the support it needs from start to finish, and once completed you are ready to tackle the next challenge with equal amounts of enthusiasm and spirit.

Senior managers are unique individuals. It is impossible to create a checklist of experience or qualifications required to be successful in this field, partly because the most important element of successful management in the arts and media is personality. Wherever you work your success will be measured by the impact you have on your organisation and that in turn will depend on your approach and the way your fellow employees relate to you. You may have read every management book under the sun, attended all the right courses and know all the jargon, but it will be your own enthusiasm for the art form or media you are working for that will enable you to inspire and lead the rest of the organisation.

Duncan Sones – CEO of the arts National Training Organisation (NTO)

Duncan Sones always felt that he wanted to work in the arts but did not think he had the talent to do anything particularly creative. At school he could see his friends desperate to go off into the artistic world, putting on plays and performing music, but Sones couldn't see how they were going to make any money out of these activities. Moreover, since his contemporaries weren't interested in the business side of the industry it appeared they were none the wiser as to how they would make ends meet either.

Sones was interested to find out how these two sides of the equation could fit together, but had no way of finding a suitable position that would cash in on that interest. Nor did his careers teacher who, when Duncan suggested he might become a curator in an arts gallery, simply told him not to be so stupid. As a result, Sones spent the first year of his employment as a trainee estate agent. It didn't take him long to realise this was not the career for him and he left the work to take a business studies course for the next three years.

While he admits the course was principally designed to create 'brand managers at ICI', on completing the course he fell into a job as marketing manager at a contemporary art gallery. 'Getting the job was a bit of shock', he admits, 'and they were certainly taking a chance on me.' Sones believes his appointment here to be indicative of how many arts organisations still approach recruitment – set up a large interview panel and slowly work through a prescribed series of questions. As a result, his new employers knew he could talk well, appeared to be intelligent, said he had a business qualification and an interest in art but had not proven any real aptitude for the work. Sones guesses he got the job because for the duration of the interview he suddenly, and inexplicably, came across as being confident.

While working at the gallery he had a great deal of contact with the regional arts board and decided this would be a wonderful place to work. Instead of being involved with just one organisation, it was possible to work with practitioners and organisations across an entire geographical area. It was possible to specialise in one particular area of the arts and help organisations take a coordinated and practical approach to working in that area.

Second time lucky

Sones' first application for a marketing post at the arts board came to nothing, which in retrospect doesn't surprise him, since he did need more experience in the field. But having spent some time getting that experience a second opportunity arose and this time he was successful. 'That's the funny thing,' he says, 'jobs have a knack of finding you as much as you go out to find those jobs.'

Having got into the arts board, Sones purposefully went out to gain as much experience in working on different projects as possible. As a marketing manager he worked directly with arts organisations on their business development plans and increasing their profitability. He was, in effect, doing precisely the kind of work he had identified for himself back at school. One project that came his way was to take responsibility for the training portfolio run by the arts board. This led to further studies of training delivered across the arts sector and finally to working with the Arts Council itself on the development of a training strategy.

At the time the sector's own training organisation appeared to be on its last legs, suffering from lack of direction and focus. Sones was given the job of assessing whether it would be better to create a new National Training Organisation from scratch or to try to overhaul the organisation as it stood. On balance, he decided the latter would be the most cost-effective option.

Training and networking

Having worked extensively on studying the state of training in the sector and with full knowledge of how the organisation needed to be taken forward, Sones was appointed chief executive of the newly recognised National Training Organisation (NTO) for the arts, otherwise known as Metier. Under his leadership, the NTO has gone from an annual turnover of a quarter of a million pounds to four times that amount. It is now responsible for setting the standards of vocational qualifications across the sector and, through research and reports, it identifies and promotes training activities throughout the sector.

'Networking is immensely important in this industry – not just for getting jobs, but for doing your job effectively', says Sones. 'It's a skill you learn and one which took me ages to develop.' Sones admits to spending a lot of time at social and formal occasions standing at the back of the room as far away from the really important people as possible. However, he says, 'I learned that if you have something intelligent to say, then you can go ahead and say it – it's quite likely other people think it too and it immediately establishes communication with new people.'

Certainly in Sones' area of work, where he may be dealing with someone from an arts organisation one minute and talking to the Minister for Culture the next, communication skills and self-confidence are extremely important. But he's also keen to stress that the nature of the sector means there is little exclusivity between practitioners in any area of the industry: 'What's interesting is that the sector doesn't have the professional associations that exist in other sectors – there are no real entry requirements or membership fees. It's a cheap and inclusive network, so if you don't go out and do the networking you only have yourself to blame.'

In terms of gaining the post of chief executive at Metier, Sones notes his path has been a matter of chance as much as it has of hard work in the relevant sectors. Certainly he could never have envisaged such a post when he started out on his career, and yet his experience and interests appear to have naturally led to this position. He notes one other very important consideration to remember when taking on a job at this senior level: 'The best advice I was given about managing an organisation is that you can try too hard to be liked. Sometimes it is necessary that you are disliked. You can be as nice as you like but you have to make sure people respect your position.'

6 Key skills and how to get them

When it comes to training and the acquisition of key skills, the arts industry can be described as 'front loaded'. In other words, the vast majority of arts employees will learn the skills they need for their profession at the start of their career. They will undergo formal training – through college, university or vocational training – and then take their first job. From this point onwards training activities severely reduce and practically all new skills are acquired on the job. There may be some vocational training for the individual from time to time, but in general all their time will be dedicated to work. It is certainly rare that anyone takes a career break to learn substantially new skills or to undertake another significant period of learning.

One of the chief barriers to individuals seeking new skills or trying to improve their current ones is the working culture within the industry itself. With so many organisations under pressure in terms of time, funding and resources, devoting time to learning is extremely difficult. If you are able to sit around and study, you're clearly not working hard enough. If an organisation does recognise it needs new skills, it may be easier for that organisation to bring in a specialist who can immediately do the job, to outsource the work to a specialist organisation or simply to get an employee or someone on work experience to do the job, learning as they go. All of these options remove the need for an organisation to invest in an effective training package or to wait for an individual to develop new skills before bringing them to the organisation. There is a considerable challenge, therefore, to everyone working in the arts to improve their skills while maintaining steady and secure employment.

Making the grade

There appears to be a strange attitude towards qualifications within the arts sector. Since there are no straightforward well-worn paths to the top artistic jobs, the importance of qualifications to securing success is by no means clear. It appears that high-flyers who are well qualified believe that their qualifications have little to do with their success, while those with few qualifications believe people who do want to succeed stand a better chance of doing so if they are highly qualified. This phenomenon may signify nothing or simply go to underline the fact that there is no direct relationship between qualifications and success, and that high flyers tend to attribute their own success to chance and fortune rather than any other factor.

All this muddies the waters of how to gain key skills relevant to the sector. While there is no doubt that certain skills are required for success, there is no set way of gaining those skills or proving you have them. The good news is that the sector is certainly not anti-training and in many areas training activities and opportunities are improving as organisations realise the benefit of developing management and administration skills internally. However, given the precarious situation of many arts organisations, financing a long-term training and succession programme is the last thing on their agenda. There are ongoing initiatives to address this, not least from Metier, the arts sector's national training organisation, which is seeking to promote continuous professional development throughout the arts sector. Nevertheless, it is still the case that individuals must be proactive to get the skills they need for success rather than waiting for useful courses to come their way.

In the media sector there is more certainty. Once again, greater definition to employment structures and clear company hierarchies mean that it is easier for employees to identify moments when they experience a significant step up in their career and therefore need extra training to fulfil their new role. In addition, the secure financial footing afforded by large media companies can mean there is an established training programme supported by a strategic personnel management function. In this way, emerging talent can be identified and individuals will be developed through the organisation according to their aspirations and the needs of the business. There may be training, coaching and mentoring initiatives that any employee is entitled to in order to help the organisation plan effectively for the personnel requirements of the future.

Getting the basics

The media also has a strong tradition of training and development. The idea of the trainee cub journalist dates back many years and still exists today. Everyone is expected to start at the bottom, perhaps in the local or regional press, where they learn the basic journalistic skills – shorthand, typing, reporting and researching. They can then build on that experience and improve their skills as their career progresses. It is interesting to note that even within the new media channels – the information services run via Internet, WAP or digital TV – the onus is still on recruiting people who have these professional journalism skills. To do otherwise would be to bring a liability into the organisation. The employee may have fabulous ideas with regard to content and style but if they do not have those basic skills or an understanding of how to go about researching and writing a story, they will not be able to perform effectively under pressure. As soon as deadlines appear or pressure increases, the employee may fail at a very basic level.

While generally requiring innovative and inspirational people to lead arts and media organisations, it is clear that in many cases organisations promote and appoint like with like. In other words, the editor with a background in local news reporting will recognise the value of a writer with that background and therefore feel safe bringing them into the organisation. A press and publicity officer who has had experience of working in a provincial theatre will have a clear idea of the kind of skills and experience amassed by someone who is working in a similar role. If you are to achieve a high-flying career in the arts and media you need to impress the people who already have those roles and the only way to do that is to build a strong

CV that demonstrates that you have taken your career seriously and that you have the skills and competencies recognised as crucial by the industry.

These kind of skills are also crucial if your networking activities are to be successful. Sceptics may tell you that success is simply a matter of who you know and not what you know and they can point to a whole host of incompetent or poor-quality arts workers who have enjoyed success that far outstrips their talent. This may be so, but these people have been successful in part because what they have delivered, in spite of its quality, is precisely what the people who employed them wanted. Their immediate employer may well have initially contacted them for the job because they knew them, but there is a difference between bringing in a friend to do something and bringing in someone who you know has the skills to deliver what you want. In other words, yes they got the job through personal contact, but that personal contact was supported by proven and reliable skills. No one in a position of authority is going to put their own career at risk by working with a complete unknown who can offer no proof of ability.

Thinking big

If you find yourself working within an organisation where training is a low priority and there seem to be few opportunities to further your skills you must take the initiative to continue your learning. Many high-flyers recommend that any first job should be taken with a large organisation. It is not simply that these employers are more likely to run training and development programmes, but working in these organisations will mean there are people around you from whom you can learn. Watching the work of a senior fund-raiser will tell you more about the work and the sector than trying to make up the role for yourself as a single worker in a small theatre company, for example. Employment in a large organisation may mean you start off with menial work and low levels of responsibility, but you will have the opportunity to discuss the work with those around you, and possibly even find your own mentor or coach who can help you develop your career.

Taking the coach

Those working in small organisations may find they have greater levels of responsibility and a wider area of work, but they will also have less chance to learn from the work of others. In this instance, the best move is to find someone who can provide a mentoring or coaching role just to ensure you are still exposed to new ideas. It is easy to throw yourself at an admin or lower management job with all the energy and enthusiasm you have, but you risk wasting your energies if what you do is ineffectual. You also run the very real risk of career burnout, seriously damaging any prospect of future promotion or advancement you might have. Unless you take a measured and sensible approach to running your career – tackling the work and specific challenges in a professional and methodical way – you are unlikely to survive in your profession. Too often, highly talented people, whether a performer or a manager, run out of ideas or simply stick to repeating what they did before, which means that inevitably they will be left behind as the industry moves on.

Finding a mentor or a coach need not be difficult. Identify someone in your own organisation or who works in a similar organisation in a senior position. They need not necessarily be holding the job you aspire to, but they will have a great deal of experience in the sector on which they can draw, and a clear view over the arts or media sector you are working in. Alternatively, you may be able to source such support through your regional arts office. These organisations can be the source of a great deal of support for your career. They will know what specific training is available and may even be able to help finance training activities. They will certainly be able to provide a channel through which you can contact suitable high-flyers who are open to the idea of acting as your mentor or coach.

If you do get a mentor or a coach, use them well. They are not there to tell you what to do with your life but to provide an informed view on your career. They are a sounding board, possibly suggesting different approaches to a problem you are dealing with or offering advice on ways to gain new skills and experience. Whatever the level of their support it is up to you to be proactive – to use them for the advice you need and to ensure they remain focused on what you want, and not just on subjects they know.

The importance of support

Whatever your organisation, it is imperative that you receive support from somewhere because the structure of the arts and media industry is such that as your career progresses you will be faced with significant new challenges every time you receive promotion. Since arts organisations are often small in size, the steps up between one job and another can be significant. You may go from working as an assistant in a press office to having sole responsibility for running an entire press office. Such a move could mean you are then responsible for managing the work of two or three other members of staff, ensuring they are able to complete their work to required targets. You will need to delegate work and exercise effective personnel management. You will need to motivate your staff, discipline them where necessary and even solve problems for them without letting them feel they have failed. All this is a huge change from simply being responsible for your own work.

A similar step change exists in the media. There is a huge difference between being a contributor or straightforward journalist and taking editorial responsibilities. It is a significant change from having responsibility only for delivering your own material to managing and editing the contributions of others. And since journalism itself is such a hands-on activity it can be extremely difficult to let go of that side of the job and adapt to more management-driven targets. Within TV and film production a similar shift exists between having direct responsibility for the practicalities of making the film or programme and having responsibility for overseeing the making of that programme – and of making other programmes in the series. Taking on an executive production role such as this requires the ability to take an overview of the programme and exert influence through the work of others. You can't wade in there and do it yourself, you need to motivate people to move in that direction. The trick is to ensure you have the right skills ready for when you make the move, and that is either a matter of finding specific training courses that will develop those skills or of gradually assuming those kinds of roles within your working life.

In the world of TV, for example, you may find that while working as a producer on one programme for a production company you are able to be involved at a more executive level on another show. You might be able to expand your responsibilities in creating a film to include a higher level of decision making and influence. Alternatively, you may come up with an idea for a series that, if accepted, means you will take executive responsibility, rather than simply working on making the show. Similarly, in the print media, you may be working as an editor but come up with an idea for a new publication. Realising this publication could lead you into publishing management under your current employer's organisation, or you may decide to set up the publication independently. Once again, this development is a matter of using the skills you have to move further up the hierarchy within your profession.

The demand for skills

Within the arts industry there is a constant demand for workers who have the right experience and skill levels to take on more senior roles. The high step between administrative roles and senior management means individuals can find themselves stuck at the lower level unable to achieve new and significant responsibilities. With limited training resources available within organisations, the result is a dearth of candidates with the skills required to secure promotion. Moreover, in some organisations, external consultancies and specialists are used to carry out certain tasks, making it impossible for lower-level managers to get the experience and skills they need to progress.

You can speed up your promotion, therefore, by ensuring you have the right level of skills at the right time. You must be proactive and find the jobs that will give you the skills and experience you need. This might mean finding a professional course, that covers the area you want to work in. It might even mean transferring out of the arts sector for a while to gain a new level of work experience and responsibility before coming back into the sector at a higher level. By taking such actions to develop your own skills you can improve your chances of promotion and of securing a high-flying job.

Management courses

In some areas of senior management it is clear that the only way to gain the skills required is through standard management courses such as those taken by managers in all sorts of commercial operations. There are many managers in the arts sector who have taken business-led qualifications, such as HNDs and even MBAs, in order to sharpen their business skills. There may initially be a feeling that the arts world is simply too different from the world of commerce to benefit from these courses, but at the end of the day you will need skills ranging from effective time management through to understanding and operating financial plans and budgets – activities that are no different from those carried out in other industries. One senior manager compared these training activities to the 'warm-up' exercises of actors and performers. There's no way a musician, actor or singer would walk out on stage having just arrived at the venue, and immediately start performing. They will carry out a few exercises to start off with, and perform sound checks, voice exercises and so on, before starting the performance proper. In the same way, fund-raisers, administrators, press officers and other managers can 'warm-up' their skills before starting on the work in hand.

Business-related courses are of increasing relevance to arts organisations as the links between the arts and business grow stronger. Even if you still maintain that managing an arts organisation is entirely different to running one in manufacturing, because you understand the reasons behind corporate actions and the models on which they make their decisions, you will find it easier to communicate with these organisations and to attract sponsorship or their support in the future. This is particularly the case in the area of fund-raising. Understanding what businesses want and what they can gain from working with the arts is key to attracting their long-term involvement.

Within the media industry, some organisations offer their managers refresher courses to ensure they maintain a high level of performance. Editors may take courses on press law – a subject that is in constant flux and open to reinterpretation, requiring senior editors to constantly keep pace with developments. There may even be courses that support editing or writing skills – offered not because the individual is deficient in this area, but because this new input could inspire a greater performance from the individual. Once again, if these kinds of courses are not supplied internally as part of your job, you should seek similar support for yourself.

Strategic skilling

As you progress through the industry, you should make sure your skills become more strategic and more specialist for your particular area of work. Many senior managers in the arts and media industry have found that due to pressure of time and work it is simply impossible for them to keep pace with the progress and use of technology. In TV production, for example, advances in recording and editing technology means it is a full-time job just to keep up with all the various types of studio equipment in use today. Internet and WAP (Wireless Application Protocol) technology is changing monthly, making it impossible for senior editors concerned with the management of day-to-day content to keep up to date. Senior-level managers are therefore caught in a trap – desperately needing to know and understand the capabilities of the new technology but not having enough time to find out about it.

The answer to this is to find the right balance between relying on the one hand on your own knowledge levels and on the other on the opinions of people around you who have a closer relationship with the technology. To some extent, it is more important that you have excellent inter-personal skills than technology skills, because it means you can communicate effectively with the technology-oriented staff who do have the best technology skills. In this way you will still know what the technology is capable of and how best to exploit that capability for your organisation. You will then be able to make management decisions about issues such as how much to invest in the technology, and what other resources are required in terms of personnel or content to make that investment pay. Such awareness can be crucial to successfully guiding a media organisation in the right direction for the future. Becoming bogged down in the details or, worse, simply ignoring the fact that the technology is moving forward will not result in success for the organisation.

Specialist versus generalist

The choice between gaining specialist or generalist skills for working in the arts world can have a crucial influence on your value in the workplace. A specialist journalist who concentrates on political coverage, or a media manager specialising in new technology or Internet programming, may be able to increase his or her market value through that specialism. Knowledge will always be in demand, so if you can make yourself the ultimate resource on a particular subject you will attract employers in a way the more generally skilled worker would not. This is not to say that one is more valuable than the other, simply that you should understand your own skills, eg are you naturally a specialist or a generalist and how does this correspond with the employment market in which you are operating?

Within large organisations there is a place for both the specialist and the generalist. You would employ specialists, for example, to take care of personnel policy, or to manage the Web site technology or marketing. In each area of the organisation you'd find a highly skilled person, who may even have specific professional qualifications and membership of appropriate organisations to demonstrate their level of professionalism in that area. They might be qualified chartered accountants, or members of the Chartered Institute of Personnel Directors. In the centre of this organisation would be a more generalist senior manager – a person whose skills lie in coordination, strategy and team motivation. This generalist will certainly have a background that includes one or more specialist positions, but they will have developed and demonstrated the skills required to hold the whole organisation together, to ensure each department works in harmony with the others to move the organisation forward.

Specialism and the creatives

Specialism is particularly important if you want to be a high-flying creative. If your main aim in life is to be a pop star you need to be able to deliver your particular product in the best way you can whenever you are required to do so. You need to be completely dedicated to that one activity. Your training should reflect this and you should gain the necessary skills that area requires – music, voice and performance skills. Professional classical musicians spend entire days practising their instruments – a clear illustration of how concentrating on specialist skills is key to success.

If you want to be a professional writer there are all sorts of ways you can improve your skills. Joining local workshops or signing up to nationally run initiatives will improve your skills. There are a whole host of presenter-orientated courses for radio or TV hopefuls. Acting courses may be taken on a full- or part-time basis and are widely available across the country. In each case, if you are determined to be successful in your particular field, then make sure you are highly skilled in that field and ready to meet the challenges that such work entails. The same applies for those who want high-flying jobs in marketing, personnel or other specific areas of arts management. Identify the area you want to work in and then concentrate on securing the skills and qualifications necessary for that work.

Developing your skills

It is only through developing a high level of specialist skills that you can attain a high-flying position in areas such as journalism, film production or editing without having to take on a senior management role. These workers need a high standard of specialist skills because it is only through these skills that they can gain some job security. They have no 'in-house' training scheme or personnel department to look after them, so it is up to the workers themselves to maintain their position in the industry. This requires a mix of proven abilities together with constant investment in their own skills. A film editor, for example, must ensure they are aware of developments in the technology used for film editing because by doing so they increase their employability. The journalist who specialises in political stories may take a specific politics-related course or undertake dedicated personal study in that area in order to understand the subject fully. Indeed, some high-flying managers in the media industry suggest that it is far better for someone intent on becoming a journalist to gain a first degree in an unrelated subject and then to take the vocational press qualification, rather than taking a general media degree in the first place. If the individual were to take, say, economics and then do a journalism course, they would be in an excellent position to start working as a political journalist – having both the specialist knowledge and the vocational skills required.

The smaller an organisation, the more responsibilities each manager will have and therefore the more generalist they will need to be. In the case of generalists it is better to gain as many skills and as much experience across a variety of management roles and arts or media organisations as possible. Managers are fairly mobile across the industry and getting a wide range of skills will make you far more attractive to employers looking to bring in someone with fresh ideas and a new outlook. Gain your skills and training from as many different sources as possible and always look for points of cross-over – where an idea from one area of the industry can be applied effectively to another area with positive results. To be a good generalist means having a wide range of management skills but combining this with a passion for the arts sector or media in which you are working.

Key skills for management

Self-reliance

One skill required by high-flyers in the upper reaches of arts and media organisations is that of self-reliance. As an effective manager you have to remember that you can't always be everyone's friend while working with them. Being a manager means taking hard decisions – ones that may not be popular and that could even lead to other people losing their jobs or undergoing substantial changes in their working lives. The arts world is portrayed as being very chummy and soft, but this does not mean managing arts and media organisations is fun and games from start to finish. These roles are tough and, as mentioned before, may not be as well recompensed as similar roles in other industries. You have to accept that in these jobs you can't be friends with everyone all the time.

Creativity

Creativity is a prime skill requirement within the sector throughout the management levels of arts and media organisations. While other parts of industry may take a more macho approach to problems – channelling financial resources to meet a challenge or swiftly creating task groups to address certain issues – managers within the arts industry rarely have those kinds of resources. They need to find more imaginative and low-cost solutions to their problems, which may require their organisation to change its way of working, rather than simply looking for more resources or finances to help remedy the situation.

Creative management also means challenging people within your organisation and industry rather than simply allowing them to blindly follow established processes. Audiences for both arts and media want to see development in the products and services they receive. They want to see innovation, whether that be in delivery platforms or the style of delivery. The industry is extremely sensitive to audience trends so must always be one step ahead of the game, partly leading the audience towards new developments, partly responding to audience demands. It is impossible to do this effectively within an inflexible structure. Good management is therefore not simply tied to increasing efficiency or improving performance, but to creating the right environment in which creative teams can work.

Managing discontinuity

One other skill all successful arts and media workers share is the ability to work with and manage discontinuity. Wherever you are working, whatever you do for whatever organisation or company, it is likely that the project you are working on will last for a limited number of weeks or months before you have to move on to work on something entirely different. You may continue with the same organisation, but the people, resources and objectives of your next project are completely different to the previous one. Managing discontinuity means that you are able to go from managing a writing festival, for example, where a series of events occur in one location over a number of weeks, to arranging an intensive two-week UK tour by an international writer. It's the same job, using the same skills but with entirely different resources and a different focus.

Qualifications versus experience

Interestingly, some high-flyers in the arts and media industry have risen to their positions with little or no formal education or qualifications. Naturally, there are the celebrities – the people who were in the right place at the right time, who were recognised to have talent and who were able to build this talent and good fortune into a successful career – but there are also those who are now reaping the benefits of a lifelong career spent with only a few employers, learning skills on the job and taking promotion as opportunities occurred.

The chance of gaining a lifelong career with one employer – even with the BBC – is extremely unlikely today. The industry is too fragmented and amorphous to guarantee anything like that. However, what is important to glean from people who have had a reasonably straightforward career is that their skills have been developed through gaining an instinct for their work rather than going out and becoming academically trained for the industry. With so many media courses and qualifications available today, the value of one course over another is extremely difficult to argue. In any case, there is a world of difference between knowing the theory behind TV or film production and actually being able to do it in practice. Ultimately, therefore, the best way to achieve the skills you need is to go out and practise in the area you want to work. This applies to directors, programme makers, actors and all creatives, but it also applies to potential managers. The only way to find out if you have the interpersonal and organisational skills top-level managers need is by making yourself available to take on those management roles. You could find yourself volunteering to organise an arts festival, or to manage the work of a theatre company or music group. It is only by doing the job that you will discover how well equipped you are for the work, whether it is the job for you, and the skills you need to develop to be successful.

7 Where to find a top arts and media job

Within the useful contacts listings in the Appendix, you will find details of the main publications that carry appointments information and job adverts. However, it is a fact that the majority of top jobs within the arts and media are never actually advertised to the public at all. Being in line for a good career opportunity usually means you are already known to the organisation trying to appoint someone, or, more likely, you work for them already. Within large organisations certainly, the more senior appointments are made from staff already working for the organisation rather than going to the trouble of bringing someone in from outside who will need to learn how the company works before they can start contributing to that work.

Having said that, it is still possible to find your job through the pages of the industry press, and even through a job advert. It may seem ridiculous, but even creatives can get their break this way. The idea of advertising for the position of pop star may have seemed ridiculous at one time but now, thanks to acts such as Take That, The Spice Girls and Hear'Say (from TV's *Popstars* programme), one of the easiest ways to achieve fame is to win an audition for a purposefully assembled, managed and marketed pop act. If it's simply celebrity you want, there are other TV programmes you could search out. Some of the successful contestants in *Big Brother*, for example, went on to be offered presenting and performance work. Having said that, it now seems clear that, as the programme slips into the past, they will end up with something less than their allotted 15 minutes of fame.

Industry- and media-related publications do carry opportunities for creatives who do not want to sacrifice their own individual creativity to achieve their artistic aims. Musicians, pop groups, writers and actors can all find opportunities through publications that advertise competitions, auditions or talent-finding initiatives that may be key to gaining recognition for the work that you do. The BBC recently ran an extensive talent initiative that included a search for children's TV presenters, DJs, stand-up comedians and sitcom writers. At any one time they may be running different initiatives, on the lookout for certain creatives, perhaps in the field of drama writing or even to discover new live bands.

There are a host of literature prizes and awards that are open to all comers, whether currently published or not. *The Writer's Handbook*, published annually by Macmillan, contains extensive listings of prizes available to writers of all genres, sometimes offering substantial cash prizes, but more importantly, bringing recognition and status to the winner.

Finding a manager

For many creatives, be they artists, musicians, performers or writers, the key to finding a top job rests in securing an agent or manager who will find career opportunities and make sure their clients are considered for those opportunities. Sometimes gaining a manager or agent seems like a catch-22 situation – they may not be interested in your work until you have achieved some level of success in the area of your work, but you can't achieve that level of success until you've got an agent or manager who will put you up for the right kind of work.

In some cases, finding a manager can be straightforward. The manager of a pop group, for example, may be one of the band's friends – someone who takes care of booking the gigs, publicising the band and other functions on behalf of the performers them-selves. Of course, the more knowledgeable the manager is about their area the better, but for bands who are just starting out, having a friend who'll take care of that side of operations will be better than nothing. In addition, the novice manager can concen-trate on learning about the industry and how to promote the band while the act themselves concentrate on creating the music.

A good agent or manager gives a creative worker a level of cred-ibility that is harder for the creative to achieve on their own. Having an agent doesn't guarantee work – just as having an agent doesn't mean you will always produce fantastic work – but it does mean that someone else has an interest in your success. Someone else is batting for you and is in a better position to see the opportu-nities open to you. The work of the agent or manager puts them in touch with the wider arts world – they will be aware of TV or theatre productions in development, they'll know when films are slated to be shot. If they are good, they will have direct contact with casting agents, music publishers or programme production companies and be ready to put you forward whenever it seems appropriate.

Getting an agent or manager is a matter of impressing that indi-vidual with your talents. The only way to do this is by performing, writing or creating something you think they will be interested in. You need to turn in well-attended and successful gigs, you should storm the show with your acting talents, you should produce a piece of writing that is clearly commercial. Ultimately, you need to convince your agent or manager that by engaging in creative activity you will be able to make money because it is your work that will bring the agent or manager money. Unless you can deliver, no amount of promotion or development by an agent will bring you success.

As you become more successful you may decide you need a new manager or agent to represent you. You should not feel bound to the agent or manager who orchestrated your first break. Different agents have different contacts, they are able to negotiate different deals. If you feel your work is becoming more valuable, you should find an agent or manager who reflects that increased value and will ensure that value is consistently realised.

Promoting yourself

All workers in the arts sector – not just creatives – need to be good at self-promotion. Just as it is unlikely that anyone would ask a complete unknown to take the starring role in a high-profile theatre performance, it is unlikely that anyone will be asked to be head of marketing for an arts organisation if they have not already shown their talents and expressed their determination and desire to take that position. It is easy to see how a musician might market themselves through playing their own gigs and publicising the event to the public and the industry. But how might a marketing assistant or magazine editor do the same within their role?

Networking

The answer is a combination of networking and communicating your own enthusiasm for the work. If you can demonstrate your ability and motivation, your employers will take note and be aware that they should either give you more responsibility or face the fact that you could leave the organisation in order to find new and more satisfying opportunities. Successful networking means talking to people outside your employing organisation to keep in touch with opportunities that exist in the wider industry sector. It is likely that you will know people who work in a similar situation to yourself and through these contacts you can discover if there are any opportunities emerging. There may be talk of a new project for some company, or someone higher up a different organisation is about to move on, creating a suitable opportunity for you. This kind of information will be crucial for you to identify where next to take your career.

The amount and quality of opportunities can depend on other factors within the industry. In the broadcast media, many companies depend upon programme commissions from the BBC to provide the company with work. As a result, there can be periods of time when there are few opportunities around because everyone is waiting for the commissioning decisions to be made. Once they are made – whether it be for radio or TV – the successful production companies will then start recruiting personnel to work on those programmes. The majority of these people – producers, directors, editors and even researchers – will be working freelance or on short-term contracts for the company. Therefore, to be successful these workers need to ensure they are in touch with other people in the industry. They need to know when the commissions will come through and be ready to offer their services to those who might employ them. The same situation occurs in film making. It is only by being in the loop – knowing what's happening within the industry – that you will be ready and available to take the high-profile work when it becomes available.

Key publications

The key to gaining these opportunities is to keep abreast of developments through the industry press. Industry publications are therefore not simply useful for the recruiting advertising they may carry but for the general industry information they offer. The TV industry press will tell you which production company is involved in which programme, who is responsible for getting crew to work on those productions and how active the company is at any given time during the year. With this level of information you can be proactive and approach companies to offer your services at precisely the time they are looking for you.

Similarly, within the print media the industry press is a useful guide both for direct recruitment and for indicating areas where you might be able to find work with a higher profile than you currently enjoy. The _Press Gazette_ covers all developments within the print media, while new publications covering e-business, multimedia and Internet developments frequently carry details of new media ventures and areas where lucrative employment may be found.

Industry publications can mean more than what appears on your newsagent's shelves. _Ariel_, the in-house magazine at the BBC, for example, carries opportunities that do not always receive extensive advertising in the external press. This publication can be found in most BBC centres. You may find other in-house publications – from unions and representational organisations – that enable you to tap into future deals and developments and find a way to further your own career.

The Internet offers another chance to enjoy the benefits of networking and to source opportunities to attain high-profile work. There are a wide range of resources on the Net, all of which will help your career, whether it gives you a chance to promote your own work, to hear about vacancies as soon as they happen or just to keep up with industry news. There are Web sites that will give you inside information on a particular employer or organisation, sites that discuss the future development of the arts, and mailing lists that enable people with similar interests to discuss their work, share ideas and inform each other of employment opportunities.

Location

One final subject that should be discussed in this chapter is your own location. From this book – the case studies and the listings in the Appendix – one may get the impression that in order to have a top job in the arts or media one can only work in London. Many of the case studies have moved to London in order to work, and many of the organisations listed are London based. While there is a thriving industry outside London, there is no escaping the fact that being in the capital will significantly raise your chances of getting a high-profile job in the arts and media. Clearly there are significant and very important companies and organisations throughout the UK where you can enjoy a high-flying job in this industry. However, simply because of its size, the capital has more publishing companies, television companies, theatres and galleries than any other location in the UK. With a larger potential audience for arts events and a huge consumer market for the media, there is a greater range of arts and media organisations in the capital – there are fringe theatres, galleries and specialist publishing houses that simply could not function anywhere else.

The capital is home to the major nationwide media services, as well as institutions such as the National Theatre and the Arts Council of England. West End theatre shows have an international reputation and when a film is premiered in the UK it usually happens in London. The capital also has an extensive arts network and there are many private and public clubs where arts practitioners meet to discuss their work and to network. Given this, it is clear that there are far more opportunities to work in the arts and media sector in London than in any other location in the UK. Moreover, because of London's status, even if you are working at an assistant level – for a theatre box office, a business magazine or a book publishers – your job is likely to have more profile than if you were carrying out that same work in the provinces.

Ultimately, while it is more than possible to have a high profile and lucrative career in the arts and media industry anywhere in the UK, it is likely that at some time you will need to work in London to prove your skills and gain the high profile you deserve. Even if your career is based entirely outside the capital and you rise to be chief executive of a regional arts office, for example, you will still find you need to travel to London to carry out some of your work. In this way, whether you are a creative, an administrator or a senior manager, it will be difficult to establish your high level of success until your work has been recognised by the arts and media industry in London.

Appendix: Useful addresses and Web sites

Useful organisations

ACQUIS
Web site: www.acquis.org.uk/careers_uk/careers_uk.html – International Web site with jobs and careers information for the theatre, based on Royal National Theatre personnel.

Arts Council of England
Web site: www.artscouncil.org.uk/ – Jobs page, comprehensive directory of grants and awards plus information on applying for funding.

Arts Council of Northern Ireland
MacNiece House, 77 Marlow Road
Belfast BT9 6AQ
Tel: (028) 9038 5200
Web site: www.artscouncil-ni.org/ – as above, for Northern Ireland.

Arts Council of Wales
9 Museum Place
Cardiff CF10 3NX
Web site: www.ccc-acw.org.uk/ – as above, for Wales.

Association for Business Sponsorship of the Arts (ABSA) – now known as **Arts and Business**
Nutmeg House, 60 Gainsford Street, Butlers Wharf
London SE1 2NY
Tel: (020) 7378 8143
Web site: www.aandb.org.uk – This organisation promotes the cross-over of business with the arts, facilitating the sharing of skills as well as encouraging sponsorship and financial support schemes. Events programme and information on training courses.

BBC
Web site: www.bbc.co.uk – Extensive site on BBC's output including Jobs and Talent sections under 'At the BBC' heading. The first of these links to useful career resources, the second to the BBC's ongoing search for new creative talent.

BECTU (Broadcasting, Entertainment, Cinematography and Theatre Union)
111 Wardour Street
London W1V 4AY
Tel: (020) 7437 8506
Web site: www.bectu.org.uk – News, Skillsbase training and careers information, plus extensive links to other industry resources.

British Film Commission
Web site: www.britfilmcom.co.uk – Principally set up to promote the UK as a production centre for films, the Web site includes useful links to other film-based networks, production companies and funding sources.

British Film Institute
21 Stephen Street
London W1P 1PL
Tel: (020) 7255 1444
Web site: www.bfi.org.uk – News, features and facts on the film industry. Links to _Sight and Sound_ online magazine, and to education and funding resources.

British Films
Web site: www.britfilms.com – The film and TV department of the British Council, includes catalogue of British films and of international film and video festivals.

British Phonographic Industry
Web site: www.bpi.co.uk – Resources include careers and employment structures, opportunities, links to record label sites and information on publications including 'How to Set up a Record Label'.

Channel 4
Web site: www.channel4.com – As with the BBC, this site includes job pages with current vacancies.

Director's Guild of Great Britain
Web site: www.dggb.co.uk – Trade Union for directors in TV, film and theatre. Publications and links to other organisations and interest groups.

English Regional Arts Organisations
Web site: www.arts.org.uk – This Web site includes a directory leading to regional arts organisations (known as regional arts boards prior to restructuring). Information can be found on how regional arts are supported, training and development initiatives plus jobs and other links.

Equity – Actor's Union
Guild House, Upper St Martin's Lane
London WC2H 9EG
Tel: (020) 7379 6000
Web site: www.equity.org.uk – Actors and performers' union, site includes news and events as well as membership information.

The Film Council
Web site: www.filmcouncil.org.uk – Strategic agency to develop film industry in UK. Site includes funding and general industry information.

Musician's Union
60 Clapham Road
London SW9 0JJ
Tel: (020) 7852 5566
Web site: www.musiciansunion.org.uk – Union for professional musicians. Includes industry news and practices, as well as useful links to further resources.

National Union of Journalists (NUJ)
Acorn House, 314 Gray's Inn Road
London WC1X 8DP
Web site: www.gn.apc.org/media/nuj.html – Web site maintained by the London freelance branch, includes industry news and links.

Networking for Women in Film, Video and Television
c/o Vera Media, 30–38 Dock Street
Leeds, West Yorkshire LS10 1JF
Tel: (0113) 242 8646
Web site: www.networking-media.org

New Playwrights Trust
Interchange Studios, 15 Dalby Street
London NW5 3NQ
Tel: (020) 7284 2818

Northern Ireland Film Commission
21 Ormeau Avenue
Belfast BT2 8HD
Tel: (028) 9023 2444
www.nifc.co.uk/ – A development agency, this site gives training
resources and production news.

PACT (Producers Alliance for Cinema and Theatre)
Web site: www.pact.co.uk – Trade organisation for TV, film, animation and
new media companies. Job page and publications page including 'Art of
the Deal' – a guide to business affairs for film and TV producers.

Royal National Theatre
Web site: www.nt-online.org/home.html – Current and future productions, plus education resources.

The Royal Television Society
Web site: www.rts.org.uk – RTS events includes seminars such as 'So You
Want to Be a TV Presenter'. Links to other broadcast organisations.

Scottish Arts Council
12 Manor Place
Edinburgh EH3 7DD
Tel: (0131) 226 6051
Web site: www.sac.org.uk/ – Site gives information on Council's activities,
publications, funding and useful links.

Scottish Screen
249 West George Street
Glasgow G2 4QE
Tel: (0141) 302 1700
Web site: www.scottishscreen.com – Promoting film, TV and multimedia
in Scotland. Site includes training, funding and other resources.

Sgrin, Media Agency for Wales
The Ban, 10 Mount Stuart Square, Cardiff Bay
Cardiff CF10 5EE
Tel: (02920) 333300
Web site: www.sgrin.co.uk – Developing skills and entrepreneurial
activity in the arts world. Training and funding resources are featured on
the Web site.

The Society of Authors
84 Drayton Gardens
London SW10 9SB
Tel: (020) 7373 6642

The Society of Authors in Scotland
Bonnyton House, Arbirlot
Angus DD11 2PY
Tel: (01241) 874 131

South West Media Development Agency
59 Prince Street
Bristol BS1 4QH
Tel: (0117) 927 3226
Web site: www.swmediadevagency.co.uk/ – Funding and development
body for film, TV and related projects. News and useful resources
featured on site.

The Writer's Guild of Great Britain
430 Edgware Road
London W2
Tel: (020) 7723 8074
Web site: www.writers.org.uk/guild/ – Web site contains news and
specific interest areas such as books, films, radio and writers' resources.

Places for work

Listing directories and industry adverts. See also publications listed in
'Keeping up with the Industry' below for publications with job adverts.

film-tv.co.uk – Web site: www.film-tv.co.uk
– Opportunities listed for film crew, jobs and online directory.

The Knowledge directory – Web site: www.theknowledgeonline.com
Also published as *The Knowledge* in print form by:
United Business Media Information Services, United Business Media Ltd
Riverbank House, Angel Lane
Tunbridge, Kent TN9 1SE
Tel: (01732) 377041
– Huge industry reference catalogue of resources throughout TV and film
industry, including jobs and training.

Spotlight – Web site: www.spotlightcd.com
Also published in print form as *The Spotlight*, this the industry-used
directory of actors and performers.

The Stage – Web site: www.thestage.co.uk/jobs/
– Opportunities listed in all areas of theatre work.

UK MEDIA – Web site: www.mediadesk.co.uk
– News, funding, events and information for film, TV and new media.

Publications

Arts and Books – Saturday supplement to *The Daily Telegraph* newspaper.
Media – Tuesday supplement to *The Independent* newspaper.
Media Guardian – Monday supplement to *The Guardian* newspaper.
Media Times – Friday supplement to *The Times* newspaper.
Willing's Press Guide, published by:

Hollis Directories
Harlequin House, 7 High Street
Teddington TW11 8EL
Tel: (020) 8943 3138
– Comprehensive directory of all press publications – magazines, periodicals and newspapers.

The Writers' and Artists' Yearbook
A & C Black
35 Bedford Row
London WC1R 4JH
Tel: (020) 7242 0946

The Writer's Handbook
Macmillan
25 Eccleston Place
London SW1W 9NF

Keeping up with the industry

Useful addresses

Department for Culture, Media and Sport
2–4 Cockspur Street
London SW1Y 5DH
Tel: (020) 7211 6000
Web site: www.culture.gov.uk/ – Overview of government policy and action on supporting the arts sector.

Emap Media
Web site: www.emap.com – Home page of the Emap group, including links to their magazines, radio, specialist TV and interactive media products, plus job opportunities.

FutureNet
Web site: www.futurenet.co.uk – Home page of the magazine publishers, includes jobs listing.

Useful publications

Ariel (the BBC's in-house magazine)
Room 123, Henry Wood House, 3 Langham Place
London W1A 1AA
Tel: (020) 7765 3623

British Film Institute Film and TV Handbook
Facts and figures and thousands of contacts from the BFI (BFI, 21 Stephen Street, London W1P 1PL; tel: (020) 7255 1444).

Broadcast
Emap Media
33–39 Bowling Green Lane
London EC1R 0DA
Tel: (020) 7505 8000

Press Gazette
Quantum Publishing
19 Scarbrook Road
Croydon CR9 1LX
Tel: (020) 8565 4200
Web site: www.pressgazette.co.uk – Site includes news, features, jobs and training opportunities.

Screen International
Emap Media
33–39 Bowling Green Lane
London EC1R 0DA
Tel: (020) 7505 8102

Sight and Sound
BFI
21 Stephen Street
London W1P 1PL
Tel: (020) 7255 1444

Stage, Screen and Radio
BECTU
111 Wardour Street
London W1V 4AY
Tel: (020) 7437 8506

The Stage and Television Today
47 Bermondsey Street
London SE1 3XT
Tel: (020) 7403 1818
Also, visit their Web site: www.thestage.co.uk

Televisual
Centaur Communications Ltd
St Giles House
50 Poland Street
London W1V 4AX
Tel: (020) 7970 4000

Training resources

NB. Training resources are also available through the Arts Council and regional arts offices, plus publications listed under 'Keeping Up with the Industry'.

Arvon Foundation
Totleigh Barton, Sheepwash, Beaworthy
Devon EX21 5NS
Tel: (01409) 231338
Web site: www.arvonfoundation.org/index/
Residential creative writing courses for everyone.

Edinburgh Film Workshop Trust
56 Albion Road
Edinburgh EH7 5QZ
Tel: (0131) 656 9123
Web site: www.efwt.demon.co.uk

Focal – Web site: www.focal.ch
European site devoted to training in film industry, audio visual and multi-media.

FT2 – Film and Television Freelance Training
4th Floor, Warwick House, 9 Warwick Street
London W1R 5RA
Tel: (020) 7734 5141
Web site: www.ft2.org.uk

London College of Printing
Elephant and Castle
London SE1 6SB
Web site: www.lcp.list.ac.uk

Metier
Glyde House, Glydegate
Bradford BD5 0BQ
Web site: www.metier.org.uk

National Council for the Training of Journalists
Latton Bush Centre, Southern Way
Harlow, Essex CM18 7BL
Tel: (01279) 430009
Web site: www.nctj.com

The National Training Organisation for the Arts and Entertainment Industries
National Film and TV School
Beaconsfield Studios, Station Road
Beaconsfield, Buckinghamshire HP9 1LG
Tel: (01494) 671234
Web site: www.nftsfilm-tv.ac.uk/

National Training Organisation for Broadcast, Film, Video and Multimedia
Ty Newydd Writers' Centre
Llanystumdwy
Cricieth, Gwynedd LL52 0LW
Tel: (01766) 522811

The Northern School of Film and Television
Leeds Metropolitan University, 2 Queen Square
Leeds, West Yorkshire LS2 8AF
Tel: (0113) 2831900
Web site: www.lmu.ac.uk

Screenwriters' Workshop (Formerly **The London Screenwriters' Workshop**)
114 Whitfield Street
London W1P 5RW
Tel: (020) 7387 5511
Web site: www.lsw.org.uk

Skillset National Training Organisation (NTO)
2nd Floor, 103 Dean Street
London W1D 3TH
Tel: (020) 7534 5300
Web site: www.skillset.org

Management training

Cranfield School of Management
Cranfield, Bedford MK43 0AL
Tel: (01234) 751122
Web site: www.cranfield.ac.uk

London Business School
Regent's Park
London NW1 4SA
Tel: (020) 7262 5050
Web site: www.london.edu/

Manchester Business School
Booth Street West
Manchester M15 6PB
Tel: (0161) 275 6333
Web site: www.mbs.ac.uk

Index

Page references in *italic* indicate figures or tables